Manifesto for Learning

Also available in the series:

Creativity in Education edited by Anna Craft, Bob Jeffrey and Mike Leibling

Differentiation in Teaching and Learning by Tim O'Brien and Dennis Guiney

Promoting Quality in Learning by Patricia Broadfoot, Marilyn Osborn, Claire Planel and Keith Sharpe

Manifesto for Learning

Janet Collins, Joe Harkin and Melanie Nind

continuum
LONDON • NEW YORK

CONTINUUM
The Tower Building, 11 York Road, London SE1 7NX
370 Lexington Avenue, New York, NY 10017-6503
www.continuumbooks.com

First published 2002

British Library Cataloguing-in-Publication Data
A catalogue record for this book is available from the British Library.
ISBN 0-8264-5097-0 (hardback)
ISBN 0-8264-5096-2 (paperback)

Typeset by CentraServe Ltd, Saffron Walden, Essex
Printed and bound in Great Britain by Bookcraft (Bath) Ltd, Midsomer Norton

Contents

Acknowledgements

We are indebted to all the people who have helped in the development of our thinking over the years, particularly Carol Dale, Trevor Dawn, Georgina Glenny, Dave Hewett, Kieron Sheehy, Janet Soler and Gill Turner. Our colleagues at the Open University, Oxford Brookes University and elsewhere have been hugely influential. We are grateful, of course, to Francis, Rebecca and Lindsey for their care and emotional support. We would also like to thank our editor, Anthony Haynes, for his invaluable support and encouragement, Kathy Hall and Bridget Hoad who provided constructive, critical comment on early drafts of the manuscript, and Bronwen Sharp and Shereen Benjamin who supported us in the final stages of preparation. Most of all our thanks go to teachers and learners we have worked with and been inspired by, who are too many to mention by name.

Preface

The initial impetus to come together to write this book came from each of us reading and hearing about the others' work in the field of communication and the social and emotional aspects of teaching and learning. Our backgrounds, prior to working in education departments in higher education, and our continuing primary interests are in different phases and types of education. As a former primary school teacher, Janet Collins is now involved in the professional development of teachers. Joe Harkin's background is in further education and in the teaching of English. Melanie Nind's history is in special schools, in particular in teaching students with severe learning difficulties. The more we became aware of each other's work the more we were able to identify some common themes and a clear sense of a common message. It is this common message that we share in this *Manifesto for Learning*.

The literature on learning is extensive and multifaceted. Research in education has often been context-specific, often with a failure to make connections between different domains. The result is that the promotion of good learning often begins to feel either tightly defined or unmanageably complex. It is easy to lose sight of the bigger picture. Drawing on our research and experience, what strikes us is that good learning depends crucially on a few straightforward, easily understood principles. This is true irrespective of the age or the nature of the learner or indeed the context in which they are learning. What we discuss in this book is these principles and the challenge of applying them. In brief these principles are that good learning should be:

- transformative
- active and interactive
- intrinsically motivating and
- lifelong

Moreover, good learning takes place in the context of:

- nurturing relationships and
- rich communications

We believe that by grasping these principles and acting on them, we as teachers can improve the quality of learning throughout education.

Here we briefly introduce ourselves individually in order to share our personal investments in the issues we raise together in the *Manifesto*. By outlining the research we have done, often with other colleagues, but not each other, we show what each contributes to the collaboration that has resulted in a far greater shared understanding of good learning.

Janet Collins

In common with many teachers, I believe that my views on teaching and learning were first influenced by my experiences of being a learner in primary and secondary school as well as at university. During my own education I was privileged to be taught by several intelligent, enthusiastic and highly motivated individuals who cared as much for their students as they did for the subject they taught. Under their tutelage I witnessed learners, myself included, grow in knowledge, skill and confidence. Thus I entered the teaching profession with a firm belief that learner confidence and warm, caring relationships were at the heart of good teaching and learning.

Teaching for nearly a decade in mainstream inner city primary schools, I worked with many pupils who were deemed to have acute emotional and behavioural difficulties. Over the years I learned, through trial and error, observation and reflection on experience, a range of strategies that helped me to anticipate, reduce and deal with potentially violent and abusive behaviour and language. The support and encouragement of colleagues was central to my ability and willingness to cope with the stresses of the job. This affirmed for me the importance of warm and trusting relationships in education. Indeed, to this day a fellow teacher, Carol Dale, continues to be a close friend and confidante.

My career and professional interests took an unexpected turn when I began to analyse my pupil's participation in whole class discussions. For the first time in my career I began to pay particular attention to the pupils in my class who were relatively quiet and who did not demand attention from their teacher or other staff (Collins, 1993). A longitudinal study, which explored the educational, social and emotional needs of the quiet, seemingly compliant pupils in my class, was subsequently published (Collins, 1996). In this study I shadowed these pupils through the final two years of their primary education and their first year in secondary school. In common with much of my subsequent research, this study involved semi-structured interviews with pupils, parents and teachers as well as participant and non-participant observations. The findings of this study are referred to at intervals throughout the *Manifesto*.

Having left teaching to complete the research I then began a new career as a contract researcher in Sheffield and Leeds Universities and the Open University. My role as a contract researcher involved me in work in a range of areas including bilingual education (see, for example, Harrison and Collins, 1998) and the use of ICT in schools (e.g. Collins *et al.*, 1997; Collins and Syred-Paul, 1997). It also provided me with the opportunity to carry out a number of projects that highlight the social and emotional aspects of learning. The first of these, *The Life Histories Project* (which began in 1996), involves follow-up interviews with those who had taken part in the original study as well as an analysis of interviews with adults who self-report that they were quiet at school. These interviews provide graphic accounts of the ways in which individuals' self-perceptions and behaviour are coloured by experiences of feeling themselves ignored by teachers in school. This led to a consideration of habitually quiet non-participatory behaviour: as a form of exclusion (Collins, 2000b); the need to respect and develop learner confidence and self-esteem (Collins, 1994, 2000a); and the need to match curriculum and teaching style with the needs of less vocal learners (Collins, 1997). More recently I have been involved in working with teachers to help them to identify and empower quieter pupils in their classrooms (see, for example, a first report of *The Participation in Schools Project* in Collins and Marshall, 2001).

As a lecturer in education in the Centre for Curriculum and Teaching Studies at the Open University I currently supervise on the EdD and MA programmes. I recently led a team that produced an MA module for primary teachers entitled 'E842 Developing Practice in Primary Education', which highlights many of the themes and issues discussed in this book. I believe collaboration with colleagues during the writing and teaching of that course is helping to shape both my thinking and my practice. I would like to thank all my colleagues for the direct and indirect influence they have had in the writing of this book.

Joe Harkin

I am Reader in Education in the Institute of Education, Oxford Brookes University. Previously I have worked in higher and further education elsewhere in England and abroad. I have a particular interest in and experience of the education of young adults, by which I mean people of roughly ages 14–24.

My specialism is English and Communication, although my first degree is in Economics. This fact is pertinent because I have always felt uncomfortable with the way in which you have to choose 'subjects' during formal schooling. In the last sentence, the word 'choose' should also be in inverted commas because there is often very little real choice involved. For example, absurdly, at 14 I had to choose between History or Geography although I wanted to study both, and between Art and Wood-work when I wished to study neither. Whilst we have moved away to some extent from such rigid choices, it remains true to say that 'subjects' constrain the learning journey of many people.

As an educational researcher, my learning journey has taken

me through a desire to improve the language skills of young adults, in order to equip them better to study and to assert themselves. I was lead consultant in England in a project looking at the development of communication skills. This was frustrating in two major respects: first, the development of language skills is a *process* that implies changes to the practice of education in classrooms; and not, as interpreted by government, another '*subject*' to be added to an already crowded curriculum. Second, it was clear that many teachers were locked into such dysfunctional equilibria with young adults that they found it almost impossible to change their practices, even if government policy made this feasible.

My frustration led me to explore ways, through the *Communication Styles* project (Harkin *et al.*, 2001), of helping teachers in a process of *self-directed* professional development *with* their learners, with the potential to develop more equitable relations in formal education between learners and teachers. These new relationships would be marked by a wider repertoire of language use, which would approach more closely normal adult-to-adult interaction.

Arising from this project, I co-directed a European *Quali-teach* project to find out the views held by young adults in different countries of what characterizes a 'good' teacher (Harkin, 1998a). Both the *Communication Styles* project and the *Quali-teach* project showed how important to effective education is the quality of the relationship between teachers and students. The process of education is vitally important and unless this is well founded upon supportive relationships many learners will not succeed in becoming 'lifelong learners', especially if the 'subjects' they are studying are not personally meaningful to them.

My research led me inevitably to more philosophical issues about the nature of human experience in the contemporary world (Harkin, 1998c, 2000) and to the formulation of a position that emphasizes that fundamentally there is more that unites human beings than divides us. Through a critical awareness of the forces that seek to divide us, we may seek better ways of being together in community. One important aspect of community is formal schooling and this therefore led to the concerns articulated in this book. Working with Melanie and Janet has shown me once again that, despite the different focuses of our individual research, we are united at a much more profound level of human experience and endeavour.

Melanie Nind

At the crux of my earliest teaching and throughout much of my research has been a concern with facilitating fundamental communication development. My first teaching post was within a long-stay hospital for adults with severe/profound learning difficulties. The students at our hospital 'school' were pre-verbal and often at pre-intentional stages of communication development. Many of them had additional sensory or physical impairments and had behaviours and difficulties in relating that placed them on the autistic spectrum. My challenge was how to go about teaching something useful to young people who did not know how to make eye contact, to communicate basic needs and to share space with others. This focused the mind beautifully on some of the bigger questions in education – what are we aiming for? is this curriculum meaningful? how can I proceed without getting to know these learners?

This introduction to teaching thankfully led me down a very fruitful path. It led to an awareness of the power of collaborative problem-solving with colleagues as we shared our concerns and anxieties and took risks together in trying new approaches. We came to mistrust much of the mechanical approaches of behavioural methods popular in special education at the time. Instead we favoured the implicit interactive pedagogy of caregiver–infant interaction in which fundamentals such as eye contact, turn-taking and joint focus are learned spontaneously in the context of rich and playful interpersonal exchanges. The teaching approach of *Intensive Interaction* that evolved is well documented (see in particular Nind and Hewett, 1994) and is referred to at intervals throughout the *Manifesto*.

My research has focused on whether this approach works (Nind, 1996) and with whom (Nind, 1999; Nind and Powell, 2000). I have looked at the nature of interactive approaches, their concern with process over product and the fundamental principles of the learner being active, even taking a lead, whilst the teacher is responsive and attuned (Nind, 2000). I have critiqued approaches that seek to normalize learners rather than respect diversity (Nind and Hewett, 1996; Williams and Nind, 1999). Most recently I have been looking at inclusive pedagogy and found the interactive principles, which involve continuously adjusting the teaching to feedback from the learner, to fit well with inclusive philosophy (Nind and Cochrane, in press). By working with Janet and Joe, whose work is with verbal and more able learners, I have been able to reflect on how far some of my working principles as a teacher, which have grown from my particular set of experiences, can be applied more widely.

*   *   *

The nature of our collaboration in writing this book has helped to illuminate some of our working principles – the need for trust and acceptance; the need for intrinsic motivation; the pleasure and challenge of co-construction of meaning. It has also sometimes underlined the difficulties, particularly the gaps between what we hold as ideal and the compromises we make in the context of restrictions placed on us, particularly of time for leisurely pondering of that which is important to us as teachers, as learners and as people. In this book we assert that relationships are fundamental to learning and we share some of the interpersonal qualities and behaviours at the heart of this. We are each involved in various kinds of teaching at a distance in which we strive to make connections with our learners. Much of the writing of this book was also done at a distance, using what we know about connecting to make this work. We confess, however, that our most enjoyed times were those face-to-face meetings in which we enjoyed the process of open communication and temporarily lost sight of the product.

We begin the book with our understanding of the nature of good learning and how it can be fostered in Chapter 1. In Chapter 2 we consider the characteristics of learning in infancy and how these provide a model for good learning for life. We go on to look at how learning is enhanced through warm reciprocal relationships in Chapter 3. A breakdown in such relationships is one of the features of communication breakdown. Chapter 4 considers what we mean by a breakdown in communication and the various processes at work when this happens. Chapters 5 and 6 look at learner and teacher perspectives. Together they show the complexities of the interrelationship between these and their importance for fostering good learning. Collaboration amongst learners and teachers is the theme of Chapter 7. In Chapter 8 we go on to develop this theme of collaboration in a discussion of learning communities as the context for good learning. Discussion of communication styles within learning communities is explored in Chapter 9. We conclude with our 'Manifesto for Learning' in Chapter 10.

Chapter 1

What Is Our Understanding of Learning?

In this book we seek to share the understanding we have gained as learners, teachers, researchers and collaborators about the nature of learning and in particular about what we see as good learning. We are concerned with learning that is 'owned' by the individual, that is meaningful to them and that enhances their feeling of self-worth and their personal power. We hold in esteem a learning process that is active and interactive, set within the context of warm and nurturing relationships and rich in communication. We contend that this kind of learning is valid irrespective of the age or ability of the learner, or of their learning context, though we acknowledge some cultural differences. We recognize our bias in writing from our perspective as teachers in an English (higher) education system and we attempt to make explicit where cultural dimensions are relevant.

Throughout the chapters that follow we describe what we understand by good learning in more detail, using examples from a range of educational settings and age-phases to illustrate the principles we contend are key to this learning. First, though, this chapter foregrounds the key ideas in the book by introducing our understanding of good learning, outlining some important extra-pedagogical factors in learning that the book will and will not address, and opening the discussion of what can be done within our sphere of influence as teachers to foster good learning.

What are the aims of education and good learning?

Discussion of what constitutes good learning must relate, in large part at least, to what it is education is aiming to do. For many the purpose of education is, and always has been, a deeply contested issue. Carr and Hartnett (1996) suggest that arguments about the purposes of education have reached unprecedented levels over the past two decades. They argue that this is due in part to the fragmentation of educational theory into so many different disciplines and so many paradigms within those disciplines, so that even the fundamental questions are contested. There is division of theory into the history, philosophy, psychology and sociology of education with their various priorities and epistemologies. There are more positivistically minded educational theorists who are concerned with how curriculum knowledge can best be organized and taught and other educational theorists who are more concerned with whose knowledge is valued and taught and the justification of criteria against which education is judged. We do not consider ourselves as within any of the education-related disciplines, but as educationalists – teachers – with a particular interest in what goes on in learning interactions. For us the aim of education of primary interest is the fostering of lifelong learners, who have an ongoing enjoyment of learning. We are interested in the social and emotional aspects of teaching and learning and what this can help us to be and become.

Education is always and everywhere based on values – acknowledged or not. Our values as educationalists and as people reflect our belief that there is more that unites human beings, at a fundamental level, than divides us. This is not to deny difference but to found it upon a more basic premise. We must learn to live together in community. Stress on individual consumption in a competitive and aggressive process has permeated values in education where even human knowledge is packaged as a commodity. The sad results in damaged lives are to be seen every day in our schools and colleges. This book is about an alternative vision of learning communities in which people's emotions and whole selves are valued and learning is a social process.

Transformative learning

Education is variously seen as being about socialization and social control, through the transmission of social and cultural values, and, in contrast, as about empowering learners to question, think and decide for themselves. Whilst we are reluctant to position ourselves as politically naïve in relation to these debates, we are also keen in this book to focus on ideals. Quite clearly, a range of extrinsic factors deeply affects education, including who determines the nature of the curriculum and assessment, and its resourcing and management. If education seems not to be working – measured, for example, by high levels of learner disaffection – then, according to Grubb (1999), on both sides of the Atlantic there is a tendency to resort to 'vulgar pragmatism' – a tinkering with curriculum, assessment or resourcing, while avoiding any more profound critique of educational principles or practices. Much of what we are concerned with here is what education should be about, what optimal learning looks and feels like. We do not want this to be so far removed from the everyday realities of teachers that they cannot make connections, but we equally do not want everyday realities (and the inevitable cynicism) to let us lose sight of the values we hold dear. Thus, for us, one of the features of good learning relates directly to one of the ideals of education, that is, the aim to be *transformative*.

Our notions of transformative learning and education partly derive from critical social theory, which was developed between the 1920s and 1950s by thinkers and philosophers who were influenced by Marxist theory and the struggle to challenge oppression and domination through encouraging engagement in both critical thought and critical action. In this context 'critical' implies a conscious radical intent to change society through enabling learners to become politically aware in order to give them the power to act to transform society. This theory views society as characterized by struggles for power between unequally matched groups who are contesting with each other to possess knowledge, as well as status, material resources and political power. This focus upon inequality, domination and empowerment is directly linked to an interest critical theorists show in addressing issues related to class, gender and ethnicity. We extend this critical theory to include learners with learning and other disabilities acting to transform educational communities and their own learning situations.

Making the pedagogical more political implies extending the notion of schooling to encompass a broader notion of education, so that schools and teachers become engaged in the ongoing struggle for democracy, justice and equality. Educational research which draws on this theory focuses on a discussion of the empowerment of students and the transformations which pupils and schools can undergo to become sites of 'democratic and liberating learning'.

Paulo Freire's work has been fundamentally influential in the literature related to critical pedagogy. Freire argues that the oppressed need to avoid seeing their predicament as unresolvable and become aware of their situation so they can recast it as a 'limiting situation that they can transform' (Freire, 1972, p. 33). He uses the term praxis to describe a process of reflection and action upon the world in order to transform it. Praxis is at the heart of our notion of critical pedagogy. It is the empowering set of practices, which stress the learner as a critical investigator, rather than the passive recipient of knowledge. The teacher is also cast as powerful, rather than powerless – another important recurrent theme in this book.

> To be a good liberating educator you need above all to have faith in human beings. You need to love. You must be convinced that the fundamental effort of education is to help with the liberation of people, never their domestication. You must be convinced that when people reflect on their domination they begin a first step in changing their relationship to the world.
>
> (Freire, 1971, p. 62)

Active and interactive learning

Like Freire, we believe that educators should encourage students to question and analyse their knowledge and the learning process so that they can take control and have the power to transform their lives. This relates to another of our fundamental principles of good learning; it should not only be transformative, but *active*.

An overarching obstacle to the development of a critical pedagogy is what Freire calls the 'banking model of education' (Freire, 1972, pp. 58–60). In banking education, the teacher is the subject of the learning process, while the students are objects or containers that are filled by deposits of information. The more full the container, the better the teacher. Those students easiest to fill are judged the better students, and those students who resist being filled are 'problem' students. Part of Freire's objection to banking education is that it perpetuates oppression and prevents empowerment by inhibiting dialogue and creativity. Reality is presented as something that must be adapted to rather than changed and students are presented as objects who need assistance. Like Freire we see good learning, as opposed to banking education, as much more *interactive*, with active, collaborative problem-solving and engagement.

Active and interactive learning are about empowerment, democracy and citizenship; they are about rehearsing and preparing learners to participate more fully in active democracy (see Freire, 1972; Habermas, 1978; Giroux, 1989). A more active role and more interactive relationship between teachers and learners also means more powerful 'deeper' learning. Learning involves our whole person including our bodies, minds, emotions and social relationships. We argue that good learning is enjoyable when learners experience appropriate levels of challenge and support through trusting relationships with more knowledgeable others.

The nature of the interactions between teachers and learners has been an ongoing source of tension in our profession: how much should teachers get involved? How much control can we hand over to learners and still be doing our job? Shor (1993) debates some of these tensions, arguing that a critical teacher must also be a democratic one – what credibility is there in arguing for democracy in society and then teaching in an authoritarian way? – whilst recognizing that a teacher is, by definition, an authority in authority. In good learning neither the learner nor the teacher can be controlling or passive; the teacher must facilitate the active involvement of the learner such that the learner can take an inventive role in transforming what is internalized. Some developmentalists have begun to use the term 'guided reinvention' to describe this collaborative process involving the learner and the environment.

We support social constructivist notions of learning as an active, constructive and self-directed process in which the learner 'builds up knowledge representations that are personal interpretations of his or her own learning experience' (Lunenberg and Volman, 1999, p. 434). The process is interactive as well as active in that learning is mediated first in the interpsychological plane between a person and other people and their cultural artifacts, and then appropriated by individuals on the intrapsychological plane (Vygotsky, 1978). This involves mentoring and the construction of meaning through joint activity. The process is intensely social even when others are not present because the mediation tools (often language) are constructed historically and culturally.

Motivation, relationship and communication

Transformative, active, interactive learning begins in the first months and years of life in the rich learning context of the home and interactions with primary caregivers. (Although there is much cultural diversity in child-rearing practices, early interactions are almost universally intense social learning environments.) It is our contention that this informal and often intuitive teaching and learning, outside of education institutions, is immensely powerful. There are three main reasons for this, which again illuminate our key principles in understanding good learning. This learning is *intrinsically motivating* and it takes place within the context of both warm, nurturing *relationships* and *rich communications*. As we illustrate in detail in chapter 2, the learning interactions at the start of life are full of mutual enjoyment.

When young children enter formal education they are rich, strong and powerful learners with 'the desire to grow, curiosity, the ability to be amazed and the desire to relate to other people' (Rinaldi cited by Drummond, 1998, p. 102). During what Mary Warnock (1978) called the expressive phase, children have the power to imagine – 'to see into the life of things'. These qualities that underpin all later learning are developed at home in the company of parents and significant others and, by and large, with little or no attempt at direct instruction. Children's communication, intellectual and emotional powers are set on track in what is usually a promising start for lifelong education.

Lifelong learning

The OECD (1996, p. 99), in looking at lifelong learning, identify the 'key features of any coherent strategy for continuing growth and development throughout the life cycle' as 'enriching the learning environment early on, developing a sound foundation for subsequent growth of knowledge, skills and values, and a positive attitude towards learning'. This is not a new concept, but there is growing awareness of its importance. A willingness to learn and to keep on learning was identified by John Dewey (1938) as the most important attitude that can be formed. Much of what we regard as good learning is the affective learning of the early years and we are concerned here with how this can be retained and developed throughout learners' educational careers. The remaining element that we emphasize in our understanding of good learning is that it should be *lifelong learning*. However, we are convinced that existing formal educational structures have to be changed if learners' imagination, curiosity and desire to learn are to be fostered and maintained in our schools and colleges, such that adults can be good and lifelong learners. Willes's account (1983) of what happens to children when they enter school and become pupils is powerfully illustrative of this contention:

> The minimal inescapable requirement that a child must meet if he is to function as a participating pupil is not very extensive. It is necessary to accept adult direction, to know that you say nothing at all unless the teacher indicates that you may, to know that

> when your turn is indicated you must use whatever clues you can
> find, and make the best guess you can.
>
> (Willes, 1983, p. 83)

In short Willes's summary of the primary duty of a pupil is 'finding out what the teacher wants, and doing it' (Willes, 1983, p. 138). This image contrasts sharply with that of the same child at home who may explore freely, initiate conversations with adults and engage in elaborate and sustained imaginative games in the worlds of make-believe. Even in secondary and further education, teacher direction of the learning experience is often higher than is desirable if learners are to share power over learning and become lifelong learners. Young (1992) pointed out that in much educational practice students 'are seen as individuals who must simply be made to reproduce the point of view being advanced, by whatever means seem expedient and economical. This is already well on the way to treating students like things' (p. 36). As will become obvious in the rest of this chapter and throughout our book, we want to encourage learning environments in which the learner has the physical, temporal and emotional space and freedom to develop his or her abilities through active engagement with the learning process, with the learning material and with others. As we will show, this rests on the right to develop two interlocked human capacities: to use language to express our own views of the world, as well as to receive those of others; and to form warm, mutually supportive relationships with teachers and other learners. First, though, we contrast our picture of good learning with a picture of some of the current problems in education because reflection on this shows that a detailed consideration of good learning is warranted, needed and timely.

Failure to foster good learning

A major criticism of what happens in current educational systems is that it alienates rather than motivates learners. Official figures on exclusions, truancy and success rates indicate that in many respects the situation seems to be getting worse rather than better on both sides of the Atlantic. In England and Wales, school exclusions were first sanctioned by the Education (No. 2) Act 1986 (sections 23–27). However, exclusion was a relatively rare occurrence at the beginning of the 1990s, when only 2910 pupils were excluded. Since then school exclusions have risen to become educationally and socially significant with a steady year-on-year rise until in 1996/97 13,581 pupils were permanently excluded from school. Exclusions of course are not random in their incidence patterns and there is an over-representation of boys, black students of African-Caribbean origin, pupils with statements of special educational needs and pupils 'cared for' by local authorities (DfEE, 1999b; Parsons, 1999).

Absenteeism from school is also a large and very visible problem in England and Wales and elsewhere. The official figures published by the English Social Exclusion Unit (SEU) indicate that around 15 per cent of all pupils took at least one half day off without authority and that the average time missed per absent pupil totalled five days per year for the primary phase and ten days per year for the secondary phase (Social Exclusion Unit, 1998, section 1.2) However, there is growing evidence that the official figures are a gross underestimation of the real truancy levels. Surveys involving anonymous pupil questionnaires (for example, O'Keeffe, 1994) suggest that the incidence of both blanket truancy and post-registration truancy are much greater than was believed by the schools or than is reflected in official figures. About a third of the nearly 38,000 students surveyed for the Truancy Unit's study (O'Keeffe, 1994) admitted truanting at least once during the previous six weeks. Among 16-year-olds, 10 per cent of all pupils said they were truanting at least once a week.

This disaffection with formal education can begin very early in an individual's school career. Writing about the US context, Haycock and Navarro (1988) describe a 'process of deterioration':

> Even in first grade, some youngsters will get the sense that
> something is wrong with them; that somehow they're just not
> doing things right . . . By the sixth or seventh grade, many will

not be proficient in the basic skills . . . Though still in school, they
will have dropped out mentally. Before high school graduation,
they and many of their peers will have dropped out altogether.
(Haycock and Navarro, 1988, p. 1)

According to Covington (1998) in the USA three out of ten
students entering ninth grade will not graduate from high school.
Moreover, close to 50 per cent of Black and Hispanic students
in California will drop out of school. For many who remain in
school the prospects for learning are poor, with limited achievements in literacy. The panic about basic literacy and numeracy
levels is familiar in the English system too. Although there is
disagreement about the scale of the problem, it is generally
agreed that at least one or two million British adults have
insufficiently developed levels of literacy and numeracy as the
foundation for future learning. Furthermore, the intergenerational effects of this are clear, with a very high probability that
relatively illiterate adults will raise relatively illiterate children
(ALBSU, 1995). Oxfam International's (1999) figures put this
into global perspective, showing that 150 million children start
school but drop out before they can read and write.

The reasons for the lack of intrinsic or other motivation for
children and young people to stay connected with education are
complex (O'Keeffe, 1994) and often beyond our sphere of
influence as teachers and so our remit in this book. Inter-
nationally, as well as in the UK, poverty is a huge factor. Any
crisis in schooling is likely to be linked to factors outside the
influence of school that cause disaffection (Kinder *et al.*, 1995).
Nonetheless, educational factors are also relevant. In England,
Parsons (1999) ascribes blame for increases in learner disaffection, truancy and exclusion on specific aspects of government
policy. He is in no doubt that the problem of exclusions had
been created as a direct consequence of the marketization,
commodification and deprofessionalisation of schooling.

In the UK and elsewhere teachers and academics are aware
of the 'learned helplessness' that occurs when experience of
failure reduces an individual's confidence and competence to
perform given tasks (Burnhams and Dweck, 1995). In a recent

interview conducted as part of Open University course materials, one primary school teacher talked about how children entered her nursery with enthusiasm for learning and confidence about their own abilities but that this 'can-do' mentality visibly diminished over time, with children demanding more and more support from her, saying that they 'can't do it' for themselves. In a review of research on pupils' experiences of exclusion Munn *et al.* (2000) sum up the range of feelings, from the immediate strong negative feelings of rejection, fear and injustice to the long-term fear about the effects of the exclusion. They note the angry reactions experienced at home and the boredom and the accumulation of a negative reputation reported whilst missing school.

Based on our experience as teachers and researchers, we believe that disaffection and dropout are related in no small part to inappropriate teaching (and learning) styles and to too little regard for the social and emotional aspects of teaching and learning. Moreover, our research suggests that the adoption of appropriate teaching (and learning) styles can increase the likelihood of individuals remaining connected, becoming and staying good learners. Whilst our teaching is defined and constrained to some extent by the curriculum and assessment frameworks presented by the prevailing government of the day, and by the values and needs of the wider society in which we teach, as professionals we have some scope. We have a duty to educate and care and we have a duty to create appropriate learning environments in our classrooms and to influence the educational ethos of the institutions we represent. We have to believe that we have the power to make a difference in our own classrooms and teaching situations. Thus we return to transformative learning and to what it is we need to foster to achieve good learning.

How do we foster good learning?

In sharing our understanding of good learning we have said it should be transformative, active, interactive, intrinsically motivating and lifelong. We have stressed that good learning takes place in the context of warm relationships and rich communications. All of these themes are expanded upon throughout this book. To begin this process we need to say more about the conditions for good learning.

Starting with the learner

For learning experiences to be intrinsically motivating and transformative they need to begin with, and grow out of, the learner's prior experience and perspectives. Good learning involves a coalition between what the learner and teacher bring to the situation. We learn best when we are personally involved in the subject matter and when the learning has real meaning for us. One implication of this is that the teacher is best seen, not as an instructor, but as a facilitator, who ensures the availability of leaning materials and manages the learning environment, not least by providing opportunities for active learning. We would argue that it is important for teachers to understand the learners' perspective so that the curriculum can be made interesting and relevant. Where learning is interdependent or independent, self-directed and active, learners can and must play an active role in their own learning processes.

For learning to be linked with the learners' own history and experiences teachers need to be aware of and accept the cultural capital which learners bring. This is difficult at any time but it is especially problematic when learners' experiences and beliefs are different from, or in contradiction to, those of the teachers. Education is not only about addressing the learners' own culture but should also be about extending their experiences to embrace new aspects of a wider community. Access to the cultural capital of other communities should be seen as valuable not in terms of replacing their own experiences but as a way of extending them. Sadly, current values in society mean that this is not equal. Emphasis on elitist cultures can deny learners an appreciation of their own culture.

We have some sympathy with Gardner's (1993) concept of multiple intelligences, that is, the idea that individuals have different profiles of strengths and weaknesses in different faculties or 'intelligences'. Important to this is that the value placed on each of these intelligences is socially constructed and may differ in different cultures, but with linguistic competence being most widely valued and most dramatically shared across the human species. Part of Gardner's contribution to fostering good learning relates to our greater understanding of individuals as complex, and not necessarily the same as their teachers. Teachers' sensitivities to diverse ways in which learners think, solve problems and express themselves are limited by their own notions of intelligence (Krechevsky and Seidel, 1998); how they construct the learning environment is a reflection of how they themselves make sense of the world. Thus, there is endorsement of our contention that teachers need to get to know their learners – that there needs to be a coming together of perspectives and styles.

Gardner (1997, p. 145) argues that in order to be successful individuals must engage in regular and conscious reflection about the events in their daily lives in the light of long-term aspirations, apply leverage by ignoring areas of weakness and have the opportunity to frame or construct their experiences in a way that allows them to draw apt lessons from such experiences. By comparison, for most people their compulsory education is characterized by decontextualized learning with few opportunities to reflect on the connections between what is learned in different domains or how that learning relates to out-of-school experiences. Similarly, the academic curriculum provides little opportunity for individuals to identify and exploit other strengths. A tendency to label young children as 'failures' provides little encouragement for them to learn from the setbacks and to turn defeats into opportunities.

More and more we see learning as socially contextualized, which helps us to understand the part we must play as teachers. If, as Wenger (1998) contends, knowing primarily involves active participation in social communities then we have to find:

> inventive ways of engaging students in meaningful practices, of providing access to resources that enhance their participation, of opening their horizons so they can put themselves on learning trajectories they can identify with, and of involving them in

actions, discussions, and reflections that make a difference to the communities that they value.

(Wenger, 1998, p. 10)

In liberating classrooms, teachers pose problems derived from student life, social issues and academic subjects in a mutually created dialogue. A Freirian critical teacher is a problem-poser who asks thought-provoking questions and who encourages students to ask their own questions. Through problem-posing, students 'learn to question answers rather than merely to answer questions. In this pedagogy, students experience education as something they do, not as something done to them' (Shor, 1993, p. 26). As teachers we need to avoid unintentionally bringing about, through our teaching strategies, situations in which learners adopt a passive role. Teacher-directed whole class teaching, for example, restricts the learners' contribution to the discussion both in terms of how much they say and the content of their input. It places them in the position of responding to rather than initiating discussion and compels them to follow the teacher's line of thinking. This approach clearly has advantages in terms of transmitting knowledge, but it is of limited use for teachers wishing to encourage independent and active learning. It may be easy to recognize lessons that afford considerable opportunities for learners to engage in most dimensions of active learning and lessons that are largely or totally didactic in nature. It is also easy, however, to be lulled into complacency by lessons which on the surface appear to engage learners in active learning, as the learners are busy doing things, but in which closer analysis reveals they are in fact following the dictates of the teacher (Halsall and Cockrett, 1998).

Fostering good communication

At the heart of active and interactive learning, taking place in social contexts, is communication. For each of us involved with this book, enhancing the quality of communications between teachers and learners has been central to our teaching and to our research, as we have outlined in the preface. Communi-

cations are the behaviours that tell of our emotional and intellectual responses, that inform and shape our relationships and that
enable us to be connected in the process of teaching and
learning.

The basics for the potential for social communication such as
turn taking and attention to others' intentions may be 'inborn
features of being human' (Rogoff, 1999, p. 71). We are hardwired for social communication and our earliest interactions are
all about fostering the communication abilities that will underpin
all our later learning. While we are concerned with nonverbal
communication as much as with symbolic communication, it is
to symbolic communication and classroom talk in particular that
much attention has been paid.

In the sixties Andrew Wilkinson coined the term 'oracy' and
called for speaking and listening to have more prominence in
the classroom. Since then there have been a number of research
projects which have illustrated the importance of classroom talk.
Many of these (for example, Barnes, 1979; Alexander *et al.*, 1996)
have drawn particular attention to aspects of teacher–pupil
discourse. In the UK three government-approved and -funded
initiatives (the National Writing Project, the National Oracy
Project and the Language in the National Curriculum Project)
reiterated the message that talk has a central role to play in
developing children's knowledge and understanding.

At the time of writing, Speaking and Listening continue to be
included as aspects of the English National Curriculum (DfEE,
1999a). However, there is some disjunction between rhetoric and
practice, with classroom talk being somewhat marginalized in
the panic about literacy. The 'socio-political climate' since the
late eighties has also been 'less receptive to insight into classroom
process as a source of improved teaching than to teachers'
accountability for the *outcomes* of teaching' (Westgate and Hughes,
1997, p. 125: original emphasis). A resurgence of 'traditional'
teaching methods threatens 'to relegate pupils' listening skill once
more to limited and passive purposes' (Westgate and Hughes,
1997, p. 125). Communication key skills are now a mandatory
part of many post-16 qualifications in Britain, supported in
principle by learners, teachers and other interest groups (Dear-

ing, 1996). Accepting the principle of developing communication skills is quite different, however, from implementing them in ways that will lead to their actual development. There has been no change to classroom pedagogy to allow learners to use a wider repertoire of language in normal day-to-day studying. Instead, communication skills have been bolted on as marginal additions to already crowded programmes, where they carry little formal credit. In consequence, students reject them, despite having a willingness in principle, and recognizing a need in practice, to develop their ability to communicate effectively (Hodgson and Spours, 2001). Whether classroom talk is privileged or marginalized according to the socio-cultural climate of the institution and wider context, it remains central to learning.

Fostering motivation

We have asserted that motivation is intrinsic to good learning. The role of motivation in lifelong learning is acknowledged by the OECD (1996):

> A first prerequisite, therefore, is that schools must be places where children and young adults like to be, where they experience a sense of self-worth, challenge and lasting achievement. The second prerequisite is that all children before leaving the formal educational system must have 'learned how to learn' under self-motivated and self-managed conditions.
>
> (OECD, 1996, p. 107)

Teaching can be regarded as successful only if the learners are learning. Generally speaking, for this to be achieved, the learners have to be motivated and achieve a sense of self-fulfilment though their learning experiences. They have to be involved in the learning process and they have to appreciate that the effort that is required of them is worthwhile. Where participants are ambivalent towards learning they may have an insecure or a hesitant attitude towards school and/or little confidence in their educational abilities. For many, of course, this ambivalence is due to their confidence in their own learning skills being eroded by inappropriate experiences in school. In a study of English 11-year-olds, for example, Reay and Wiliam (1999) provide a graphic account of the way in which the process of preparing for and sitting the National Curriculum Tests modified both pupil and teacher identities and practices. A growing climate of fear and anxiety had a negative effect on the confidence and performance of all the pupils regardless of their achievement levels. In addition, the pressure that children experienced also had a negative effect on peer relations in the classroom. For example, high attaining peers became the subject of serious bullying as a consequence of their getting better NCT results than the rest of the class.

Learners often feel vulnerable in learning situations, not least because of their teachers' power to control and evaluate. This affects how individuals experience learning and their openness to new experiences and ideas. A considerable responsibility is thus placed on us as teachers to reflect on how we use that power. Similarly, individual learners in a group situation can have tremendous power to control, influence and evaluate their peers in a positive or negative way. Mutual respect and genuine encouragement are likely to enhance an individual's self-esteem and motivation. Criticism and unduly negative comments about the individual or their work may well have a negative response. Irrespective of the age of the learners, teachers have a responsibility to create and sustain a positive learning environment for all, through, for example, establishing appropriate rules and ways of working, responding to rule infringement appropriately and recognizing and building on success, however small.

Within a positive learning environment we stand a chance of fostering motivation. For that motivation to be intrinsic and not just for end-goals or pleasing others, the learning experiences taking place within that environment need to be meaningful and connect with learners' lives and aspirations. We need to facilitate learners' relationship with their learning – an intellectual and emotional engagement.

Fostering emotional engagement

We have sympathy with Goleman's (1996) concept of emotional intelligence, which he derived from the work of LeDoux (1998). Briefly, this argues that we have tended to overemphasize people's cognitive skills and to underplay the importance of the emotions in learning. Goleman considers that just as education has always held a belief that cognition can be improved by a process of learning, so also can our abilities to handle emotional states be enhanced. If education does not hold a proper balance between cognition and emotion, then both are impoverished. Human beings should be viewed holistically as complex and creative users of both IQ and what Goleman refers to as EQ. Noddings (1996) holds that:

> In Western thought, affect and emotion have been distrusted, denigrated or at least set aside in favour of reason. The tendency to distrust – even deplore – emotion has been aggravated by the rise of professions with their insistence on detachment, distance, cool appraisal and systematic procedures.
>
> (Noddings, 1996, p. 435)

Research by Janet Collins (1996) and Joe Harkin (1998a; Harkin *et al.*, 2000) has shown how important the emotions are in the way that young adult learners construct their perceptions of effective teaching.

We contend that the social and emotional aspects of learning are central to good learning. Our research, experience and instincts all tell us this. A desire to connect with learners is tacit in our, and many, teachers' desire to be teachers, yet we are taught to distrust such tacit knowledge about the importance of this in teaching and learning. Thomas and Loxley (2001) are highly critical of the process in which teachers in special education have been made reliant on special techniques, and helpfully remind us that 'our humanity tells us' that children who are slower to learn need the same as any other child: 'interest, confidence, freedom from worry, a warm and patient teacher' (p. 26).

Teachers and learners need to be emotionally engaged in the process of teaching and learning, not least because 'we remember things better when we are emotionally involved' (Chamberlain *et al.*, 1996, p. 6). More importantly, thinking cannot be separated from feeling, and the emotional climate of the classroom is vital to good learning.

Fostering relationships

We believe that good-quality, positive relationships between teacher and learner matter for a number of reasons. It is through these relationships that discipline and classroom rules are established and maintained. Whilst this is especially true during the period of compulsory education, the establishment of what Hargreaves (1998) called a 'working consensus' is an important aspect at all stages of education. A working consensus is based on a recognition of the legitimate interests of other people and on a mutual exchange of dignity between teacher and learners. Embedded in this is a tacit recognition of the needs of the 'other' and a shared understanding that the 'self-image' of the other will not be unduly threatened in the learning situation.

In a learning situation both teachers and learners have the capacity to make life extremely difficult for the others involved. A pragmatic basis for negotiation thus exists. However, positive relationships or a working consensus are not automatically created. They are the result of initiatives made by the teachers as they establish the rules of engagement and ways of working together. Learners expect such initiatives from their teachers and are unlikely to challenge the teacher's right to make them, so long as the teacher acts competently and in ways that are regarded as fair. Learners by and large recognize the relative power and authority of the teacher. However, as part of the process of establishing a working consensus the teacher's power must be partially circumscribed by the understandings that are created jointly in the learning situation.

Learners of any age and attainment can be encouraged to work in a collaborative and mutually supportive environment or, alternatively, can be directed to work in a highly competitive and individualistic style. Sadly, in England at the time of writing, a number of externally imposed and centrally controlled initiatives (e.g. the introduction of Standard Attainment Tests at ages 7, 11 and 14, in addition to individual assessment at age 16, 17 and 18) make it increasingly likely that teachers and learners come to view learning in narrow, individualistic and competitive ways. This view of learning and our concept of good learning, which takes place in the context of warm and nurturing relationships, are incompatible.

Positive relationships between and among teachers and learners are important because of the way in which learning takes place. We maintain that learning occurs through communication with more experienced or knowledgeable others. Relationships based on positive regard for the other are likely to encourage learners and teachers to share their experiences, their views of the world and their (mis)understandings and thus enhance learning. Where learners understand and respect their teachers they are more likely to be motivated by the teachers' skill in, and enthusiasm for, their subject. Similarly, where there is positive regard for the learner, then the learner is more likely to be engaged in the learning process.

One excellent source of insights into the importance of relationships is the work of Carl Rogers (1983). As a counsellor, he suggested that three basic qualities are required in order to establish warm 'person-centred' relationships – namely, acceptance, genuineness and empathy. When we apply this to the learning relationship this suggests a need to receive and acknowledge learners as they are, rather than following stereotyped preconceptions or focusing on what we would like them to be. Genuineness implies that such acceptance is real and heartfelt as is our enthusiasm for the learners' individual and collective progress. Empathy suggests that a teacher needs to appreciate what the process of learning and the conditions of learning feel like to the learner. Rogers introduced the idea of providing 'unconditional positive regard' for his clients and we see this as both challenging and relevant for our teaching. Work with people with severe and complex learning difficulties reveals ways of being together in education that apply to all learning relationships:

One of the first basic steps in Intensive Interaction is to have the attitude that you will accept a student/client for what s/he is at this moment in time. You may not like everything that a person does, some of it may be annoying or repelling, but the reality is that the behaviours are not likely to stop because you find them annoying or repelling. Alternatively, much of what a person does may seem bizarre or meaningless, repetitive and obsessive . . . We now take the view that whatever a person does is likely to be meaningful to that person; it may simply be the case that sometimes we are not able to share that meaning and understanding.

(Nind and Hewett, 1994, p. 83)

Rogers' three qualities have much in common with the key attitudes of the reflective teacher. Being able to demonstrate acceptance and empathy requires 'open-mindedness' and a 'whole-hearted' commitment to the learners. It also demonstrates 'responsibility' when considering the long-term consequences of our feelings and actions. As reflective teachers we need to take account of the interpersonal climate of the learning situation and to recognize the speed with which things can happen and the inevitable power relationships between teachers and learners.

In this opening chapter we have outlined our ideas on the principles of good learning. These are developed further though-out the book. In the next chapter we focus specifically on learning in infancy as a model of good learning that should be sustained through life.

Chapter 2

Learning In Infancy – A Model For Life?

> A child begins his or her life eager and curious to know the world,
> reaching out and touching what is not understood. Sometimes it
> comes apart in their hands. The light (this light of curiosity) goes
> out as they make the inexorable march into the formal education
> system.
>
> (Crequer, 1996)

We need to acknowledge, of course, that some of the early
learning we describe is culturally specific and some is more
universal. As Woodhead (1999) discusses, it is all too easy to take
the child-rearing practices of the minority Western world as
typical, whereas experiences in the majority world might be quite
different. Many of the notions of play and interaction discussed
in this chapter are linked with Western notions of childhood and
desire for children to become independent, autonomous and
social. Research indicates that the proto-conversations and reciprocal playful dialogue may be more culturally specific, though
several of our most familiar interactive games may be found
across vastly different cultures. While we need to be aware of the
ways in which this book may be seen as culturally biased, we
also know that no teacher or learner is in a cultural vacuum.
The way in which we make sense of learning depends on the
experiences and understandings we have of the world. We
approach this book from a minority Western world viewpoint.
Our central concern is to look at learning across ages, stages and
abilities. We discuss the fundamental learning principles arising
from this perspective. To test these principles out cross-culturally
would constitute another book – with undoubtedly fascinating
debates.

Teaching pre-verbal young adults with severe and complex learning difficulties and profound intellectual impairment focuses the mind on fundamental questions of what is meaningful learning and how we can facilitate it. It was when Melanie Nind (Nind and Hewett, 1988, 1994) faced this challenge that the value of looking at the implicit pedagogy of caregiver–infant interaction became apparent. Without looking at how fundamental social and communication abilities are learned in informal settings in infancy we could not see how to teach them. In developing the Intensive Interaction approach based on a nurturing, responsive, interactive style, we came to appreciate the complexities and benefits of learning through social interaction, as typified in caregiver–infant interactions. We also came to identify fundamental principles in this learning that we saw as underpinning not only Intensive Interaction but also all other experiences of good learning that we had known, either as learner or teacher. These principles are:

- The learner is active, that is, 'a fully active participant in the activities, intellectually and emotionally engaged with the content and the teacher, making decisions, exploring and experimenting, exercising personal power';
- The learning activity is intrinsically rewarding and motivating;
- The learner shares control of the activity with the teacher.

(Hewett and Nind, 1998, p. 89)

Sharing our concern for meaningful learning for learners of different ages and with diverse abilities has involved recognizing that these and the other principles discussed in this book are fundamental to learning for most people in many situations. We argue that looking at how we first learn is helpful for thinking about how we go on to learn. Comparing the sometimes impoverished learning environment of many classrooms to the optimal learning environment of many early social interactions helps in the identification of key features and principles for learning. There is a lot to be gained, we maintain, by looking at the learning of infants, primary school pupils, young adults and more mature students and seeing, not just what sets them apart, but also what their learning has in common.

In infancy, we learn at a faster pace than we ever learn again, and yet we usually do so with untrained teachers and in relatively unplanned learning environments. Exploration of this early learning can illustrate how learning can be spontaneous and full of fun. For anyone who has taken (even a peripheral) part in nurturing an infant, much of this will make unsurprising reading. The novelty and significance here comes much more from the appreciation of this model of caregiver–infant interaction as a model that we can use to underpin all learning. Fundamental principles of learning emerge from analysis of our earliest learning experiences and these principles are readily applicable throughout later learning.

The learner is active

It has only been in the last three decades, following Bell's (1968) recognition of the two-way effects of interaction in infancy that we have been able to really appreciate that from the beginning we are active learners. Earlier models held the infant much more as a passive recipient of socializing experiences, shaped by the influences of caregivers and the environment. Babies weren't so much jugs to be filled with knowledge, as plasticine to be moulded into shape. Piaget's underestimation of the social element of learning contributed to this notion of the child as an active explorer of the world and constructor of knowledge only later when cognitive processes had developed.

Vygotsky's theories of the importance of the social dimension of learning guided research towards the social, cultural and human context in which children develop from birth. While for Piaget, development makes learning possible, for Vygotsky, learning makes development possible and that learning, particularly in the early stages, is primarily social. Studies of early infancy have shown that social interaction actually takes place from birth. (There are indications that interactions may even precede birth, but evidence here is less well developed.) Researchers have emphasized that this is *inter*action – that the infant plays an active part. Sameroff (1975) described this complex process of bi-directional influences in terms of a *transactional* *model*. The infant is influenced by the environment, but also influences it, each continuously altering the other. As developmental psychologists have understood early development in this transactional way, they have reconceptualized the infant as an equal and influential partner in the relationship.

Through this active, interactive style of learning infants swiftly become competent with complex communication and social processes. They have the essential motivation to participate and the confidence to explore. They are not fearful of trial and error nor weighed down by tight notions of success and achievement. They are actively engaged in learning processes more than actively pursuing learning goals. We argue in the following chapters that experiences of *not* being an active learner contribute to the process of becoming disenchanted with learning. The corollary to this is that to become lifelong learners we need to retain this active element. It is an anomaly that despite growing recognition of learners as active in processing and interpreting information much school-based learning is apparently not based on this premise.

Interdependence and reciprocity

Having reconceptualized the infant as active, and recognized the interaction with caregivers as the learning forum, the interdependent, reciprocal nature of this interactive context became clear for researchers. Lewis and Goldberg (1969) showed that both mother and infant had control of the interaction in 'mutual effectance', and Stern *et al.* (1977) illustrated a process of 'mutual regulation of behaviour'. Researchers strove to delineate the complexity and sophistication of the early two-way alternating dialogues. However well it has come to be understood, the two-way quality of the early interactive learning episodes is always stressed by researchers of mother–infant interaction (for example, Schaffer, 1971, 1977).

The adult role in this two-way interaction has been a continuing focus of interest for Vygotsky and Bruner. Vygotsky argued that the child is helped to move on through a Zone of Proximal Development, i.e. through

> the distance between the actual developmental level as
> determined by independent problem-solving and the level of
> potential development as determined through problem-solving
> under adult guidance or in collaboration with more capable
> peers.
>
> (Vygotksy, 1978, p. 86)

Wood, Bruner and Ross (1976, p. 90) described the adult process
of guidance and collaboration in this as one of 'scaffolding',
a very different process from direct instruction in the way
that connections between the known and the unknown are
supported.

Linked to interdependence and reciprocity, and also charac-
terizing learning in infancy, are the central features of mutual
involvement and mutual enjoyment. These features are often
connected to an element of game-playing. It is in the early games
that conversational rules of joint reference and turn-taking are
learned and practised (Bruner, 1983). The mutual involvement
and enjoyment of interactive games provide the foundation for
further interactions to proceed (Hodapp and Goldfield, 1983),
not least because they facilitate positive affect. As activities that
are child-initiated and child-maintained, interactive games
become safe and exciting environments for cognition and sociability to develop. Infant learners return to the learning situation
time and time again, actively anticipating shared participation in
meaningful, pleasurable activity.

It is easy to contrast this scenario with the scenario of later
learning (or lack of learning) in which conversational rules
enjoyably learned are often transgressed in classrooms dominated
by teacher talk, which is in turn dominated by rhetorical questions and commands. Or the scenario in which the teacher
deliberately attempts not to become too involved. There is also,
of course, the scenario in which this is not intentional, but in
which the teacher, for all sorts of reasons, fails to be responsive
or where there is no reciprocal element or mutual enjoyment.
The drive to set targets and plan tight objectives can contribute
to a learning environment that is counter to the reciprocity of
early interactive learning. Mutual trust is an important factor in

effective early learning and, by contrast, one of the features of outcome-based learning later in life is that it is a highly bureaucratized, low-trust system. Ironically and impossibly, one of its aims is to empower learners. As Ecclestone (1998, p. 18) put it, 'it is difficult to reconcile a commitment to learners' autonomy and motivation when assessment increasingly confines these to restricted choices and pre-defined outcomes'.

Interpersonal behaviours

The active, interactive nature of early learning is maintained by the interpersonal behaviours of both infant and caregiver. This may be stating the obvious, but it becomes significant as researchers begin to identify those interpersonal behaviours and reciprocal responses that are key. Ferguson (1971) highlighted the importance of mutual visual regard, mutual vocalization and reciprocated touching. Calhoun and Rose (1988) clarified that key infant behaviours have been identified as smiling, interactive responses appropriate to the stimuli, postural and gaze orientation towards the adult and vocalization. Key adult behaviours have been identified as vocalization, holding and touching the child and initiating an activity purposefully. Field (1977) stressed the role of gaze in controlling and sustaining interaction and Stern (1974) illustrated how gaze releases and elicits interpersonal behaviours in the interactive partner.

As we develop our distance, senses become more important and our reliance on touch and taste and smell less so. It is unlikely therefore, and obviously problematic, to envisage later learning being reliant on touch, or indeed some others of these interpersonal behaviours. Interpersonal behaviours, however, continue to play a crucial role in later learning (Greenhalgh, 1994). These are the vehicle for communicating our interest in our learners, our value of them. These are our vehicle for focusing and re-focusing attention, for signalling changes in pace or purpose, for showing our mutual involvement. Distance educators are acutely aware of the need for strategies to substitute for interpersonal behaviours to perform these roles.

Just as there is a whole body of literature on an optimal interactive style facilitating good learning, there is also a body of literature on interactive breakdown and interactions when one or other party has an impairment. McCollum's (1984) review of this literature highlights the fact that the establishment of mutually pleasurable interactions as the context for learning is less automatic when the infant is developmentally delayed. Without supportive feedback the caregiver can work harder at interaction, ultimately being over-stimulating and intrusive (Field, 1979). A more controlling style of interaction (Marfo, 1991) in which responses are noncontingent can result when the infant's responses are atypical and the caregiver is stressed. In this scenario the interpersonal behaviours don't 'fit' as well and the interactions become mismatched in timing and content (Carlson and Bricker, 1982). In this way the 'critical communicative match' becomes difficult to establish and maintain (Warren and Rogers-Warren, 1984, p. 63) and the 'teaching' is hampered. There is evidence that a controlling and directive interactive style is unhelpful to early learning (Hanzlik, 1989) and we have to question why it is then assumed that it can be helpful later on.

An interactive style that supports learning is reciprocally supported by the interpersonal behaviours of learners who learn well from it. It is less well supported when the behaviour of one of the parties is atypical, particularly when it is unpredictable. A broader social systems perspective illustrates how the wider context plays a part here. Helpful interactive behaviours are harder to sustain in conditions of hopelessness, anxiety and low self-esteem, but are maintained with social support (Dunst and Trivette, 1986). In later learning it is possible to examine the contextual factors that support or interfere with the effectiveness of the teaching–learning relationship, and we look at these in more detail in Chapter 3.

The responsive environment

The transition from being a pre-intentional communicator through to using language (spoken or sign) is impressive learning in any terms. Children assist their own learning of this tremendous achievement partly by eliciting a verbal environment that is helpful for them (Snow, 1976). Responding to feedback from their infants, caregivers provide a verbal environment that is structurally simple and semantically linked to the child's experience (Weistuch and Byers-Brown, 1987). They ask more questions and create 'proto-conversations' based around pauses filled with coos and murmurs (Bateson, 1979). The 'exquisite sense of timing' in which the mother 'allows herself to be paced by the infant' (Schaffer, 1977, p. 12) and the 'elaborate interweaving of their behavioural flow' (p. 5) help to ensure that the turn-taking, communing elements of effective conversation are developed and rehearsed.

At the heart of all this is contingent responding and the feelings of efficacy this generates (Lewis and Goldberg, 1969). Good interaction is dependent on sensitive and effective signalling. Indeed, responsiveness is widely agreed to be a major factor in an interactive style that is optimal for fundamental learning (Beveridge, 1989). Smith (1989) sums up what it is caregivers do in this responsive process:

> They arrange, manipulate and structure the environment in order to facilitate and maximize children's interactions. They do this by engaging in joint activities, by making use of the children's interests and inclinations, and most importantly, by being very sensitive to feedback from the children in determining what to select as the focus of joint attention.
>
> (Smith, 1989, p. 113)

One might expect learners to grow out of the need for this kind of responsiveness. One would not, however, expect them to grow out of enjoying it, or for it to cease to be effective.

Sharing control of the learning process

When we think of small infants, we may no longer think of them as passive, but we may not think of them as being in control of their own learning either. An impact of responsiveness and of a contingent environment, though, is that the infant is able to share control of the learning process. The caregiver's willingness to pick up on the infant's interests, tempo and signals means that the infant is by implication choosing and directing and learning to lead. In the beginning this may facilitate mere regulation of arousal, but from a longer term perspective it lays the foundations for later collaborative and independent learning.

Why are social interactions so important?

Clearly, some aspects of early learning occur through the infant's interaction with the physical world. It is the social environment, however, that is more salient in terms of responsivity and contingency. Mutually satisfying and reciprocal interactions play a role in developing relationships and trust and these play a motivating and general role in further development. Research on the processes of caregiver–infant interaction illustrates that the interactive processes within the infant's social world are sources of intense pleasure and powerful influences in terms of teaching and learning. The interactive caregiver plays a complex role in offering direct social stimulus and acting as a mediator of the physical environment as well offering layers of responsiveness.

Researchers have, as we have shown, begun to unravel some of the crucial elements of early interactions, but as Schaffer (1984, p. 76) argues, the 'intricate process' of caregiver–infant interaction is carried out 'so smoothly' that one is generally unaware of the diverse skills involved. This 'implicit pedagogy' (Carlson and Bricker, 1982, p. 295) has been the focus of early intervention (Calhoun and Rose, 1988; Yoder, 1990) designed to enhance the learning environment in the homes of children at-risk. It has also begun to be used for extrapolating teaching approaches which address the fundamental social and communicative development of individuals experiencing severe and complex difficulties with learning (Burford, 1986; Nind and Hewett, 1994). In this book, we examine the connections with teaching and learning at all ages and stages. Consequently, in the next chapter we explore what we mean by nurturing relationships and how these enhance learning in formal educational contexts.

Chapter 3

How Can We Enhance Learning Through Relationships?

In the preface we asserted that one of the principles of good learning is that it takes place in the context of nurturing relationships. Whilst we dwell on the teacher–learner relationship as that most within the teacher's control, our fundamental principles apply to all relationships in the learning situation, that is, relationships amongst teachers and with other staff, including managers, relationships between learners and teachers and amongst learners. They also relate to relationships between the educational institution and the learner's home and wider community.

The chapter begins with a discussion of what we mean by nurturing relationships. We then identify why we believe good relationships are fundamental to learning and discuss how relationships are established and maintained, and the pedagogic consequences for a range of educational settings.

Defining nurturing relationships

It is generally accepted that learners learn most effectively when they feel valued and secure, trust their teachers and both understand and accept the full range of classroom demands. Therefore, a consideration of the social context and emotional climate for learning is important for all learners. Both the Warnock Report (DES, 1978) and the National Curriculum Council (1989) have argued that this may be particularly important for learners with special educational needs. Using a 'transformative' rather than a 'normative' lens (Ainscow, 1999) to view such learners, however, leads us to address this priority in ways that enhance learning relationships for everyone.

Wade and Moore's (1993) research emphasizes the importance of relationships (between learners, teachers and parents) for learning. It also emphasizes the frustration and anger experienced by learners with special educational needs when their specific needs are over-emphasized or ignored. In both respects we believe that this research has clear implications for work with all learners. Richardson (1990) makes a similar point when he cites a poem by James Berry:

> I wish my teacher's eyes wouldn't
> go past me today. I wish he'd know
> it's okay to hug me when I kick
> a goal. Wish I myself wouldn't
> hold back when an answer comes.
> (Richardson, 1990, p. 97)

Richardson (1990) goes on to identify what he believes every learner (and indeed every teacher) requires, namely to be noticed, to be attended to, to be valued, to be affirmed. We believe, like Richardson, that it is out of this attention and affirmation that relationships grow and learners can develop the confidence to learn and teachers to teach.

Drawing on the work of Rogers (1983) and others, we identify the key qualities that facilitate learning as being related to relationships that are:

- Reciprocal
- Encouraging
- Loving and warm
- Authentic and accepting
- Trusting
- Empathetic

Unpacking these terms a little for work in educational settings, we interpret them in the context of professional teaching, sometimes with many learners, and with learners of all ages who bring their own predilections about these issues to the relationship.

Reciprocity emphasizes that the learner as well as the teacher can and should bring important contributions to the relationship. Even young children have an agenda and a wealth of experience to contribute and share.

Encouragement in educational settings is inevitably bound up with progress and a desire to take new steps and to do well. In reciprocal relationships both parties want this for themselves and each other. Encouragement becomes complicated by formal assessment regimes. No matter what teachers say, for many learners they know that they have to face public tests of their performance. For some learners, this may enhance their motivation to learn; others may be too scared to do their best or may be alienated by this official judgement process. Teachers have to make delicate decisions about how to encourage learners in a climate that is often designed to be cognitively and emotionally testing. This is not easy.

Love and warmth are very important in teaching people of all ages. The *Quali-teach* project (Harkin, 1998a) showed that young adult learners, in different European countries, on different types of educational programme, share very similar views of what constitutes effective teaching. The principal factor in effective teaching, they say, is warmth – shown by, for example, knowing learners by name, having time for them beyond the confines of the programme, being patient when they do not understand. This warmth is a professional love – good teachers like learners; like to spend time with them; and get as much from the relationship as they put in. Parents are aware of this too. Murray (2000), when discussing real partnerships between professionals and herself and her profoundly disabled son, stresses the need for teachers to like the child, to 'value and enjoy him' (p. 696) as the essential starting point for any learning partnership. The conditions under which teachers are constrained to work places stress on their time to get to know their learners, and good teachers, therefore, are often very conscious of the gap between their ideal practice and their actual practice. This may be harmful to professional self-esteem.

Authentic and accepting relationships are closely bound up with language use. The Gricean maxims (1975) for language use stress factors such as sincerity and truth; while Lakoff's (1977) rules for politeness include giving people room to express their own views, and equality or camaraderie: acting as though you and the person you are talking to are equal. The extent to which language use in education settings meets the normal protocols for adult-to-adult communication may be a measure of how likely it is that the relationships formed will be authentic. Authentic and accepting relationships are also about accepting the learners for who they are rather than dwelling on who the teacher might wish they were. This takes away the element of blame for being uncommunicative, working-class, attention-seeking or whatever, and places the emphasis on moving forward together. Teachers who have worked on such acceptance implicit in the Intensive Interaction approach have found it liberating (for example, Knott, 1998).

Trust in education is closely bound up with the other major factor found in the *Quali-teach* project and also in the *Communication Styles* project (Harkin *et al.*, 1999, discussed in more detail in Chapter 9), namely a range of professional behaviours that may be summarized as leadership. This is the ability to shape learning to meet the needs of the learners, the subject and its assessment requirements. This includes not just knowledge but a commitment to use this knowledge consistently in the best interests of learners. When learners sense that they are in 'safe' hands, trust follows. As in early childhood, trust is formed as a result of consistent, affirming behaviours.

Empathy, in a professional sense, is something that flows almost naturally from the set of behaviours outlined above. If you invite learners in to an authentic, warm relationship, through which trust is built, then empathy – teacher for learner – and equally importantly, learner for teacher – will be established.

Relationships are fundamental to learning

We believe, with Rogers (1983), that the facilitation of significant learning rests fundamentally upon 'certain attitudinal qualities that exist in the personal relationships between the facilitator and the learner' (Rogers, p. 121). Part of the challenge of these attitudinal qualities and the interpersonal behaviours that go with them is that we know them implicitly and intuitively but lack a vocabulary to describe them (Nind and Hewett, 2001). Bruner (1963) was aware of how little we know even about the social skills involved in an exchange of information and Stenhouse (1967, p. 63) contended that 'ideally, I suppose, teachers should have a particularly intense training "as people"', but we do not really know how to give such a training. Our training for teaching therefore tends to be specialist and academic. Here we discuss the importance of relationships for learning in terms, among others, of the co-construction of meaning, co-operation, the formation of identity and the need for appropriate levels of security and challenge.

Co-construction of meaning

The view underpinning this book is that relationships, communication and learning are immeasurably intertwined. It is through our relationships with others that we first learn how to communicate. Moreover, communication is essential in the construction of knowledge and meaning.

Communication is a highly subjective process, not least because language does not involve a simple transmission of ideas from speaker to listener or one communication partner to another. The physical signals that pass between people during communication do not carry what is ordinarily considered the meaning. Instead, they carry instructions to select particular meanings from a list of possible meanings. As a result, 'the semantic connection that ties sound-images to meanings has to be actively formed by each individual speaker' (von Glasersfeld, 1995, p. 134). As the meanings and associations are constructed as a result of individual life experiences, each communication partner brings his or her own interpretation and meanings to the communication and, as a consequence, within a group of learners, each will hold a different version of what the teacher says. Moreover, whilst language does not convey knowledge it can constrain and orient the communication partner's conceptual constructions:

The teacher cannot tell students what concepts to construct or how to construct them, but by judicious use of language they can be prevented from constructing in directions which the teacher considers futile but which, as he knows from experience, are likely to be tried.

(von Glasersfeld, 1995, p. 184)

In communicating with learners it is important for teachers to remember that: 'No-one but you can make *your* associations, and no-one but you can isolate *your* sound-image and whatever *you* conceptualize in your experiential field' (von Glasersfeld, 1995, p. 135: emphasis supplied).

It is impossible for individuals to apply exactly the same meaning to a given word or symbolic communication. Consequently, what teachers have to aim for is a situation in which their constructs and those of their learners are compatible. The communication partner who seems to understand what we mean does not necessarily have conceptual structures that are identical with ours. Understanding is always a matter of best fit rather than exact match.

To understand another's speech, it is not sufficient to understand his words – we must understand his thought. But even that is not enough – we must also know its motivation.

(Vygotsky, 1962, p. 151)

Co-operation and negotiation

It is a commonplace to state that different learners will want different things and that teachers should respond appropriately. However, giving efficacy to this commonplace is tricky. How do you gauge what different learners want? Do they really know themselves? And knowing, can a teacher respond, limited as teachers are by the requirements of tightly prescribed programmes and assessment regimes?

The *Communication Styles* project (see Chapter 9) takes these issues further and opens a conversation with teachers about the practice of dialogue with learners. We don't know if we can provide learners with what they want until we have a conversation with them and to have a conversation that is genuinely reciprocal may require the education of learners and teachers. We need to learn and practise in a process of building experience of participation and through developing the genesis of a shared language to discuss learning and teaching issues.

Between the individual and the social may be placed the communitarian, in which individuals, with others to whom they relate in a socio-emotional sense, collaborate to learn, to solve problems, to understand their circumstances, as well as to understand aspects of codified knowledge that we call 'subjects'. An important feature of communitarian views of education is that power is shared between teachers and learners.

There is a balance to be sought in education between meeting the needs of individuals and those of society. The latter, such as the need for an adequately trained workforce, may coincide to a degree with the needs of individuals; however, individual needs transcend the instrumental purposes of the state. This has often been recognized. For example, the DfEE Elton Report (1991) on discipline in schools recognized that much indiscipline comes about because the subjects imposed upon them bore young people. There must be room for some negotiation of learning goals and there must be room for negotiation of the relationship.

In empowering learners to think for themselves in the context of culturally accepted and socially determined views, we believe communication, and more specifically language, is an indispensable tool. Drawing on the work of Habermas (1986, 1987), a distinction may be made between language used for the imposition of will through power and violence and the potential of a common will formed in non-coercive communication. It is the case that much interaction in education is based on the former; however, the latter is possible and desirable.

For Habermas, the 'ideal speech situation' may give rise to a rationally founded consensus, based on a functional view of everyday language use, that what we say is comprehensible, true, right and sincere. This view of the *internal* organization of language use coincides with that of philosophers of language, such as Grice (1975), who hold that the fundamental basis for language is human co-operation, a view sustained more recently by Aitchison (1996). These views are in contrast to the popular but mistaken belief that the function of language is primarily as a conduit for information, which was countered by Reddy (1979) – this is a view of language, unfortunately, that is still prevalent in education.

Habermas argues that factors in the *internal* organization of language vie with factors of *external* organization, such as who determines the ordering of the discussion, and who can participate, and in what way, i.e. factors of power, to shape interaction. He holds that distortions in the *external* organization of language lead to systematic distortions in the *internal* organization of language. The result is pseudo-communication in which certain topics are avoided or are presented in untrue ways. The possibility of a truthful and sincere dialogue, leading to consensus, is made unlikely. Habermas never intended the ideal speech situation to be understood as a concrete utopia that would, in Outhwaite's (1994, p. 45) expression, 'turn the world into a gigantic seminar'. Nevertheless, he distinguished 'the genuinely communicative use of language to attain common goals' – which is surely the purpose of language use in education – 'from strategic or success-oriented speech, parasitic on the former, which simulates a communicative orientation in order to achieve an ulterior purpose' (Outhwaite, 1994, p. 45).

Genuine communication involves a degree of reciprocity. Thus, effective communication relates to the degree to which the participants are able and willing to respond in an appropriate way to the content and meaning within the context in which the communication takes place. Sharing a common language alone is not sufficient for effective communication. There has to be a readiness to abide by the rules implicit in each particular exchange.

A great deal of research (such as Young, 1992; Dillon, 1994; van Lier, 1996) shows that patterns of communication in formal education may be quite different from everyday communication patterns. They often do not conform to the principles outlined above in that teachers dominate the interaction. Even curriculum initiatives designed to promote greater learner interaction may not have this effect on teacher behaviour, as shown by the failure of the Nuffield Science Project to alter patterns of interaction (Egglestone *et al.*, 1976). As Young (1992) put it, in much educational practice, students 'are seen as individuals who must simply be made to reproduce the point of view being advanced, by whatever means seem expedient and economical. This is already well on the way to treating students like things' (p. 36).

It is the need to understand the words, thoughts and motivations of another that makes communication an act of relationship. The ability to make oneself understood by others, and to understand them in return, depends in no small part on the individual's sensitivity and willingness to see things from the other person's point of view. Learning is greatly enhanced if we keep in mind that the words and concepts that we use do not have a universal meaning for all. As teachers we need constantly to check the learners' interpretations and not rest until the responses seem compatible. Clearly, it is easier to orient learners to particular constructions if one has an idea of the constructions they are currently using. It is only by getting to know a learner and developing a relationship with him or her that teachers can say with confidence that they understand the conceptual portrait of that person.

Learning the language of formal education

When learners begin formal education they must learn new uses of language; this is not always obvious to either the learners or their teachers and can cause difficulties (von Glaserfeld, 1995). Much of what teachers do and say in the classroom is guided by what Goffman (1956) termed 'rules of conduct'. The way in which teachers use language and interactions tacitly presupposes the knowledge of patterns and rules that are commonplace and second nature in an adult educator's world but may be unfamiliar to a novice learner.

The following anecdotes illustrate how easily misunderstandings between teachers and learners can occur. It is reported that on his first day at school Laurie Lee was asked by the teacher to 'sit and wait in the front desk for the present'. Laurie was disappointed to discover that this did not mean he was to receive a gift. In another anecdote, from her teaching experience, Janet Collins remembers a visitor to her inner city primary school who ended his talk on the use of guide dogs by asking if the children had any questions. Vicky eagerly asked the names of all the dogs. On being told that this was not the kind of question the visitor was expecting she immediately tried again. Her second question was, 'Are you married?'

Unfortunately, as learners quickly learn what is expected of them, it is possible for them to respond to the teacher's questions in a way that covers rather than reveals a mismatch in understanding. Consider, for example, situations in which short monosyllabic answers are 'heard' by the teacher as being correct or are reconstructed by the teacher into a different answer from that originally given by the learner.

Young (1991) gives an example of how teachers can fall into habits of pseudo-communication, such as the practice of 'guess what's in the teacher's mind', illustrated by this interaction:

T   What is the reason for people writing things down?
P   So that they can give you the knowledge they have.
T   They want to give you the information . . . Sometimes it's only for enjoyment but they want you to find out something. There's a big word that means that. I'll give you a clue what it is. It begins with c.
P   Composition?
T   Very nearly. Not quite right . . . no.
P   Comprehension?
T   Well, it is comprehension . . . that's quite true . . . it is comprehension but this person is trying to carry out a method of [rising intonation] . . .
P   Communicate.
T   Good boy! Can you make it into a noun for me . . . it's a verb, communicate . . . you call it communication.
P   Communication.
T   Good boy! Communication. And that's the whole purpose of writing . . . to try to communicate with people.

(Young, 1991, p.111)

At a more subtle level, learners do not always learn exactly what the teacher thinks they should. Bereiter (1998) reminds us of situations in which two learners appear to have learned the same concepts and achieve similar scores on a first test of that knowledge. However, later, and as the work becomes more complex, one learner struggles whilst the other continues to do well. In Bereiter's (1998) terms this difference may be due to the fact that whilst both have learned the surface facts one has also learned the underlying rules and how to apply them.

Changing some of the language of formal education

Following this example through, learners are motivated to change their misconceptions when they find that such misconceptions are wrong or less than useful. This is more likely to happen through self-discovery than simply by being told. Understanding how another person thinks often involves informal conversations and out-of-classroom experiences, but it can involve the language of formal education too. It certainly involves beginning with where the learner is, what they know already, what they care about, what they are interested in. We believe we need to try to accept the reality of the learners' lived experiences and not require them to shed or deny precious parts of their identity and history at the door of the classroom. As Richardson (1990, p. 101) explains: 'these precious parts of themselves include their culture, language and dialect, and countless experiences, stories and memories of their families, communities and friends, including in particular stories of oppression and injustice'.

Building relationship and effective communication into teaching and learning, although reciprocal in essence, must be the responsibility of the teacher. To kickstart this process we, as teachers, need to begin with, not to deny, what the learner brings to the learning situation. This has clear implications for teaching and learning styles that we return to in Chapter 5. Caregivers as intuitive teachers do this automatically, and the need to work from children's interests is a golden principle of early childhood education (DES, 1990). For older or adult learners, in contrast, it is common practice to begin with a major input or keynote address from the lecturer. However inspirational this opening presentation might be, the implicit message may be that the lecturer is custodian of knowledge and the audience are empty vessels with relatively little relevant or valuable experience of their own. For presentations of this kind to be affective and effective there has to be an opportunity for learners to organize their own thoughts and to be able to make connections between what is known and the new material being presented.

Formation of self-identity

Relationships with significant others, including teachers and learners, have a major role to play in shaping the way we think about ourselves and how we construct our achievements and aptitudes. For example, learners who clearly enjoy a lesson and who respond to their teachers with interesting and relevant questions are likely to create the impression that their teacher is doing a good job. Similarly, learners who are repeatedly praised for sustained effort and interesting work are likely to believe that they are successful students. Sadly, the reverse is also true.

There is now a recognized body of research evidence (for example, Burnes, 1979; Lawrence, 1985, 1988) which reports that teaching is more effective when the teacher is able to focus not only on the development of skills or knowledge, but also on the student's affective state and on self-esteem in particular. Furthermore, the nurturing of learners' self-esteem is seen as one of the primary functions of any system of education (Indoe *et al.*, 1992; Bruner, 1996).

Lawrence (1988) offers useful conceptual definitions in which self-concept is:

> the sum total of an individual's mental and physical characteristics and his/her evaluation of them. As such it has three aspects: the cognitive (thinking); the affective (feeling) and the behavioural (actions).
>
> (Lawrence, 1988, p. 1)

This self-concept develops in three areas: self-image, ideal self and self-esteem. Self-image is defined as the individual's awareness of his/her physical and mental characteristics. Alongside self-image individuals also learn that there are ideal characteristics they should possess and that there are ideal standards of skills and behaviour which are valued within the society in which they are growing up. This is an individual's 'possible self', that which 'regulates aspiration, confidence, optimism and their opposites' (Bruner, 1996, p. 36). Lawrence (1988) defines self-esteem as the individual's evaluation of the discrepancy between their self-image and ideal self. Similarly, Bruner uses 'self-esteem' to describe a mix of agentive efficacy and self-evaluation, which combines our sense of what we believe ourselves to be (or even hope to be) capable of and what we fear is beyond us (Bruner, 1996, p. 37).

How individual learners (and teachers) judge themselves in this way is, we argue, fundamentally connected with their relationships with each other. Important to this is Harré's (1998) argument that there is no such thing as general self-esteem, but that individuals have levels of self-esteem linked to particular aspects of their life. Following this line of reasoning, if young people have low self-esteem in formal schooling, they may compensate by striving for high self-esteem in other ways. This may be through violence, early pregnancy or through achieving in a sporting or consumer culture. If schooling fails to provide young people with the means to positive self-esteem, they will inevitably seek it elsewhere.

Self-concept, of course, does not begin with formal education. According to Object-Relations theory of self, in the first instance a child's self-image and their perceptions of their ideal self are formed in the context of relationships with the mother as prime carer (Guntrip, 1949). For Guntrip (1961) 'good enough' personal relationships are those which provide age-appropriate levels of separation and attachment. They are also those in which we can be our whole selves and have complete freedom to express everything that makes us what we are. A feminist reading of this work offers a modified view of good object relationships, which further acknowledges the unique bonding that can exist between mother and baby (Chodorow, 1978), and yet does not discount the important role fathers can and increasingly do play in nurturing their children (Lewis and O'Brian, 1987).

Object-Relationists would argue that bad object relationships in childhood are internalized and become part of the child's self-image. Moreover, negative experiences set a pattern for future relationships. The extent to which self-image or self-esteem are static or fixed in early childhood is contested. Lawrence (1988), for example, argues that an individual's self-image changes over time and in the light of new experiences. Indeed, he argues that 'the more experiences one has, the richer is the self image' (p. 3). We maintain that believing that the self is open to change through learning and experience is crucial for teachers' sense of efficacy and potential; without this it is easy to accept failure as inevitable.

As schooling is one of life's earliest institutional involvements outside the family, an individual's experience of school and their relationship with teachers play a crucial role in the shaping of self (Bruner, 1996, p. 36). Consequently, there is a need for good relationships between teachers and learners in all educational settings. For adults beyond formal education, low self-esteem (and many other social problems) are closely linked to low levels of literacy, and to a lesser extent numeracy. For this reason, it is important to have accessible schemes that enable adults to recover lost ground. Furthermore, the inter-generational effects of low levels of literacy are clear – if you have low literacy, it is highly probable that your children will too, despite the best efforts of teachers (ALBSU, 1995). Most importantly then, we need to recognize that lifelong learning, like self-identity, has very early interpersonal roots that need our attention.

Appropriate levels of security and challenge

Human beings learn all the time from the moment of birth. Whenever we have a new experience we learn about that experience, about how we felt about it and how others dealt with the situation. In all these instances of incidental learning we acquire experience, knowledge and even skills without conscious effort and consequently without major risk to our self-image or ourselves.

However, the moment we enter formal education or consciously set out to learn something we have to have courage and take risks. To set out to learn something, be it learning to read, to drive a car or the subtleties of astrophysics, we have to take a series of risks. We have to admit (if only to ourselves) that we lack the necessary knowledge or skills required. We also have to admit that we are prepared to learn and risk the possible ridicule of others. Moreover, in attempting to learn we also have to accept and deal with the possibility that we might fail and the consequences of that failure or, indeed, the possibility of success. Based on our experience and research we believe that relationships with teachers and other learners can provide the appropriate level of security and challenge that is needed. Good relationships, as described above, provide a secure base from which individuals can take risks and learn.

Praise and a belief in an individual's ability to succeed play an important function here. The development of intentional communication in infancy relies on the child's caregivers or intuitive teachers imputing that intentionality (Harding, 1983). Faith that infants will become reciprocal communicators means that we treat them as such and they become such (Snow, 1976). A similar pattern applies to reading (Smith, 1978). And so on in life. The more fortunate amongst us will remember with affection times when someone's confidence in our abilities have urged us on to achieve something we had previously thought impossible.

Teachers' confidence in learners and their confidence in themselves are not of course universal. There are gender differences, well documented by, for example, Weiner (1985) and Gallas (1998), and illustrated by McCabe's (1981) example of a girl's response in a junior class questionnaire:

> Question: If you could be anything in the world, what would you choose to be?
> Answer: Secretary to a famous person.
>
> (McCabe, 1981, p. 57)

Some writers (e.g. Chodorow, 1978) argue that girls tend to be defined, by themselves as well as by others, primarily as future 'wives and mothers, *thus in particularistic relation to someone else*' (our italics) (Chodorow, 1978, p. 178). Thus, regardless of whether or not they become mothers, motherhood and a role of caring for others are central to the ways in which girls and women are defined. By comparison boys and men are more likely to be defined primarily in universalistic occupational terms. Indeed, in a patriarchal society, it is considered weak and effeminate for men to describe themselves in terms of their relationships with others.

Social class background too plays a part. The following example from Janet Collins (1996) illustrates how parent perspectives influence children's perceptions of themselves and their potential. Diana was 8 when Janet carried out the first interview during which Diana said she wanted to be a doctor. Her father clearly appreciated the value of praise in building self-confidence. There are several examples of his encouraging his daughters by praising their modest successes. However, whilst Diana's father (an unemployed painter and decorator) clearly wanted her to be more successful at school than he was, there was a limit to his aspirations for her. He could not envisage Diana as a potential doctor. To him she was 'not a go-getter'. He was surprised by, and even laughed at, her ambition:

> All she wants to do, if ever I ask her what she wants to be she says a doctor. (Laughter)
> I hope she can be but I doubt it. Or a nurse you know – I'm surprised she said doctor, there's a lot of girls say 'I want to be a nurse' and things like that . . .
>
> (Diana's father, in Collins, 1996)

It would be easier for him to accept his daughter in a stereotypical female role than as a 'trend setter'. How far this was a realistic appraisal of Diana's potential it is difficult to say. However, in an interview just before transferring to secondary school Diana did not mention the possibility of becoming a doctor but said she 'wants to help people'. Diana had already been modifying her ambition. It is tempting to suggest that she was, to some extent at least, constrained by her father's narrower perception of her. On leaving school Diana began a catering course which she enjoyed but ultimately abandoned to look after her dying mother.

Assessment regimes also have an important impact upon learners' self-esteem. As Entwistle (1987, p. 138) put it, in a 'society which stresses the importance of both academic and vocational achievements, strong feelings become associated with the judgements made of success and failure. People have to explain these outcomes to themselves.' According to a psycho-cultural theory, self-success and failure are principle nutrients in the development of selfhood. Yet the individual may not be the final arbiter of success and failure, which are often determined from 'outside' by others according to culturally specified criteria. Bruner (1996, pp. 36–7) states that school is 'where the child first encounters such criteria – often applied arbitrarily. School judges the child's performance, and the child responds by evaluating himself or herself in turn.' As recent research by Reay and Wiliam (1999) demonstrates, children's perceptions of National Curriculum assessments contribute to identity formation. In their research, the 'tension between agency and structure becomes apparent in children's differential dispositions to view the testing process as a definitive statement about the sort of learner they are' (Reay and Wiliam, 1999, p. 1). Ideally, of course, a 'good enough school', like a 'good enough teacher', should identify and reward success whilst providing opportunities for individuals to take risks in relative safety rather than, as is often the case, being 'rough on children's self-esteem' (Bruner, 1996, p. 37).

The development of self-esteem is an affective process and is a measure of the extent to which the individual cares about the discrepancy between their self-image and their perception of their ideal self. Failure itself does not produce low self-esteem but the way in which people react to the failure can do. For example, parents or teachers who do not put pressure on the child to succeed will not worry the child if they fail. In such circumstances the child is unlikely to develop low self-esteem. However, it is also possible that individuals over-generalize and, for example, begin to see failure in one aspect of their academic work as failure as a person. There is some evidence that the extent to which the views of others matter to the growing child is related to levels of self-esteem. Individuals with high self-esteem are more likely to rely on self-perception whilst individuals with low self-esteem are likely to find external sources of feedback more salient (Ilgen *et al.*, 1979).

Self-image and consequently behaviour may differ according to different circumstances. For example, learners who exhibit quiet and withdrawn behaviour in school may be far more outgoing and confident in other circumstances. Similarly, as McDermott (1996) demonstrates, the performance of individual children is greatly affected by the circumstances in which they perform, the level of support they receive and their perceptions of the task and their ability to perform it successfully. Self-beliefs exert powerful effects on persistence and mastery at a range of intellectual and artistic endeavours (Sloboda *et al.*, 1999).

Establishing and maintaining relationships

There are many things that teachers can do to foster positive teacher–learner relationships and learner self-esteem. Beveridge (1993) identifies some of these as:

- creating a climate of mutual respect;
- showing genuine interest in the learners as individuals and care and concern for the class as a whole; and
- promoting self-esteem and intrinsic motivation through the provision of relevant and achievable tasks with regular constructive feedback and praise.

All of these behaviours can be relatively teacher-centred, or relatively equitable in the sharing of power and responsibility between learners and teachers. The process of developing self-image and ideal self begins in the family and continues as the child attends school and participates in other communities outside the home. Community membership involves having various dispositions or habits of mind, which in turn contribute to an individual's self-image. It brings a sense of a certain kind of self-confidence and competence, and feelings of entitlement and empowerment (Greeno *et al.*, 1999, p. 138). This suggests that being excluded from a community can have the opposite effect. Bruner (1996), for example, draws attention to the fact that America alienates enough black ghetto boys to land nearly a third of them in jail by the time they are 30. Similarly, in the UK much time and resources are currently being spent in trying to reduce truancy in schools (Social Exclusion Unit, 1998, p. 1). The experience of learners whose feelings of exclusion are expressed through quiet, non-participatory behaviour remains an under-researched area (Collins, 2000b).

The need to achieve balance between necessary intimacy and appropriate distance is inherent in establishing and maintaining all relationships and is of particular importance for teachers and learners. Harrison (1976) described the difficulty which teachers may experience in bringing their 'authentic loving selves' to relationships with learners. He suggested that the often-expressed need to maintain a 'professional distance' implies a recognition of the difficulty in achieving teacher–learner relationships that avoid confounding a caring approach with possessive attitudes. He also acknowledged that the learner–teacher relationship might be further complicated if the teacher becomes aware of unresolved anxieties of their own which they may try to resolve through the teaching relationship. Intimacy versus appropriate distance tensions are less rehearsed but equally important for learners entering into relationships with their teachers.

In a patriarchal society independence and separateness are associated with masculinity and are valued over the 'female traits' of dependence and connectedness. However, given that self-realization grows out of relationship with others, the connection between independence and dependence is clear:

> A lack of either intimacy or appropriate distance prevents healthy development in the growing child. However, it is hard for individuals in our culture to realize that true independence is rooted in and only grows out of primary dependence.
>
> (Guntrip, 1968, p. 268)

The relationship between independence and connectedness was emphasized by R. D. Laing (1959). Laing (1959) argued that an individual who has a sense of their presence in the world as a 'real, alive, whole, and, in a temporal sense, a continuous person' (p. 39) acquires this strong sense of self through relationships with others. Moreover;

> Such a basically ontologically secure person will encounter all the hazards of life, social, ethical, spiritual, biological, from a centrally firm sense of his own and other people's reality and identity.
>
> (Laing, 1959, p. 39)

A secure person is not threatened by the possibility of entering into relationships. By comparison, insecurity leads an individual to become absorbed in contriving ways of avoiding or coping with possible infringement by others.

It is our understanding that it is only through relationships that an individual can realize their true potential. This will involve the freedom for an individual to express their 'true selves' and the freedom/need for concealment and privacy. The terms 'suppression' and 'inhibition' associated with the latter have negative connotations that deny the basic human need to maintain a strong and separate sense of self. But as Guntrip (1968) asserts:

> We must feel able to shut out the external world and maintain our right to an inviolable privacy within ourselves at need if we are to remain healthy persons.
>
> (Guntrip, 1968, p. 268)

Children may not want to discuss their home lives in school; parents may not want to share their concerns with teachers whom they find intimidating; teachers may want to hold some of themselves back. Relationships need to be allowed to form within the context of safeguards (see, for example, Nind and Hewett, 2001) but not be forced. They may never be the ideal they can conceivably be, but in Winnicott's (1986, p. 154) terms, they can be 'good-enough'. At the same time we can hold suitable 'ideal models' of teaching and learning relationships, which help to orientate our professional lives to better practice.

Difficulties that develop within relationships can be related to a breakdown in communication. The next chapter considers the various processes at work when rich communication breaks down and good learning is undermined.

Chapter 4

Why Does Communication Break Down?

This book is premised on the belief that rich communication between and amongst learners and teachers is a vital part of the educational process and that learners who do not have a voice in the classroom are disadvantaged. Teachers support learning by talking to learners, responding to what they have to say and forming suitable relationships with and between learners. For learners to be successful and make the most of the learning opportunities offered, it is important that they become active communicators. However, systematic observations of teaching and learning situations reveal that communication between teachers and learners or among learners often breaks down or is insufficiently supportive of learners and learning. This chapter considers what we mean by a breakdown in communication and what causes this to happen. An understanding of why communication may break down helps with the identification of potential solutions, which are discussed in full in subsequent chapters.

Breakdown in communication can occur at different stages:

- when the teacher does not perceive and treat the learner as communicative
- when the teacher/learner does not attend to what is being communicated
- when the teacher/learner does not understand what is communicated
- when the teacher/learner is unable or unwilling to respond
- when the communications of the learner/teacher are not valued

- when the teacher/learner responds in inappropriate ways
- when meanings are not built co-operatively.

These breakdowns in communication may occur as a result either of factors extrinsic to communication, such as class or cultural difference, or factors intrinsic to communication, such as the breaking of Grice or Lakoff maxims for interaction (see pp. 34–5). For example, problems may arise because the teacher dominates the interaction or because there is not sufficient politeness on the part of learners to sustain normal patterns of interaction. Extrinsic and intrinsic factors in language use are linked, and interact, so that, for example, a teacher's unwillingness to respond appropriately to a student's communication may be partly the result of class difference and socialization.

Examples of communication breakdown

The following vignettes from across our research and experience illustrate forms of communication breakdown.

'Sorry, what were you saying?'

During a Mathematics lesson in her primary school it was clear from her behaviour that Susie did not hear what her teacher was saying as he stood at the board explaining a mathematical problem. Throughout the explanation Susie looked unusually miserable. Appearing to ignore what was going on around her, she seemed to be focusing all her attention on a letter, which she turned over and over in her hand. Talking to her after the lesson revealed the cause of her distraction. The letter in question had been inappropriately addressed to Susie's mother who had left the family home years previously. Susie's anxiety about how to deal with the letter was compounded by her difficulties in trying to cope with the family breakup. Needless to say, she heard nothing of the Mathematics lesson and without further support was unable to complete the work her teacher had set.

'Never mind understanding'

A student on an Engineering course had trouble understanding a mathematical concept that the lecturer wrote on the board to be copied into students' notes. The student asked the lecturer to explain. Whether or not he was able to explain, the teacher simply said, 'Never mind understanding it, just get it down'. He went on to say that so long as he copied the formula as written, he would be able to handle the assessment. Understanding was not necessary.

'Time to finish now'

Malcolm is pre-verbal and has severe learning difficulties. He and his teacher have regular Intensive Interaction sessions in which they engage in a kind of interactive dance in which the teacher imitates Malcolm's idiosyncratic hand and arm movements. Malcolm takes the lead and the teacher tunes in and follows. He seems to enjoy the sense of agency in this and she enjoys feeling connected with him and a sense of efficacy in successfully engaging his attention. When she finishes the interaction and sits at the desk to write her record of it, he kicks furniture towards her. Analysis of video of the sessions shows her that she has not learned to communicate to Malcolm that the session is going to end, or learned how best to judge when to end it, or how to allow him to end it.

'Are you talking to me?'

Systematic observations in a variety of learning situations suggest that group discussions are often dominated by a small number of confident, not necessarily articulate individuals. Other individuals remain silent, frequently showing an unwillingness or inability to respond to either the teacher's questions or comments from peers. In large group discussions Vicky never volunteered an answer or comment. Indeed, she rarely spoke in class and seemed reluctant to ask for help even when she was experiencing difficulties with her work. When the teacher asked questions or required feedback of some kind Vicky kept her hand down and averted her eyes so as not to draw attention to herself. If she was chosen to answer she looked at the top of her desk and either said nothing or answered in monosyllables. If she did indicate that she might want to speak she invariably put up her hand just as another learner was chosen by the teacher. Vicky's body language and lack of eye contact appeared to inhibit conversation. Observing this process, it seemed that her teacher was in a difficult position. The teacher was frustrated at Vicky's lack of involvement. However, asking Vicky to speak when she had not volunteered to answer seldom succeeded, and only appeared to increase her obvious discomfort.

Hearing angst

A teenage girl on a Business Studies course was normally cheerful and polite and had a good relationship with other students and the teacher. One day, however, for no apparent reason she became sullen and withdrawn – glowering at the teacher and making sarcastic remarks. The male teacher was concerned, even hurt, but he only took the class for two hours a week, and was not the course tutor, so he felt unable to confront the student about her behaviour. He did not know what to do, so, being busy, he decided to ignore the behaviour, which persisted for the rest of the course. Her communication of her emotional state was never responded to.

The process of communication breakdown

When considering barriers to communication or the complex ways in which communication may break down it is important to emphasize that a transmission model of communication is inadequate (see previous chapter). Meanings are not parcelled up in words or coded in symbols and delivered in pure form to recipients who unpackage or decode those precise meanings. Instead, meanings are mutually constructed in a dynamic process (Fogel, 1993). The evolving meanings need to be checked and re-checked in a continuous process of feedback. This requires tremendous skill and sensitivity and a willingness to engage readily in communication repair.

Communication partners rarely have equal power and some are particularly vulnerable to having their communication intent ascribed or reconstructed such that it is unrecognizable to them. The dangers of this whenever there is a complex interpretation process (such as in Facilitated Communication) are well documented (Bunning, 1995; von Tetzchner, 1996). There have even been guidelines written recently to help staff in interpreting the communications of people with severe learning difficulties, based on the model that meanings are constructed co-operatively (Grove *et al.*, 2000).

Communication can break down in terms of the transmission of a message, but it can also break down in its function to bond us. Breakdown in the transmission of information is unsurprising in that 'in spite of the widespread view that language is primarily for conveying information, language is not particularly good at this: it is poor at handling spatial information, and information about emotions' (Aitchison, 1996, p. 25). Reddy (1979) showed that language is not primarily a conduit for information but a human attribute that shapes our perceptions of the world and ourselves. Aitchison (1996, p. 25) confirms that it 'is particularly good in social roles, at maintaining social ties and influencing others'.

Through an analysis of observations of teaching and learning situations, supported by in-depth interviews with the participants, we can begin to identify some of the complexities of the process by which communication breaks down. These are related to:

- inappropriate teaching (and learning) styles
- a lack of shared understanding between teachers and learners
- a failure to acknowledge and deal with the social and emotional aspects of learning.

In considering the process of communication breakdown it is important that we consider the issues from the perspectives of the learner, the teacher and the learning environment. Looking at the variety of perspectives in this way should prevent us from adopting a deficit model, which presupposes that the breakdown in communication is due solely to difficulties or inadequacies within the learner. In reality when communication breaks down it is usually a two-way, transactional process, involving both teachers and learners. Moreover, it usually occurs in environments that in some way are not conducive to communication.

By adopting this transactional perspective we are recognizing the bi-directional influences in communication (see Nind *et al.*, 2001, for a fuller discussion). This enables us to focus on the interface between the communication partners. The possibilities for intervention lie with either partner and the challenge and responsibility for successful communication lies with both. Having said this, teachers, as professional communicators, have the primary responsibility to shape effective communications.

Inappropriate teaching (and learning) styles

As identified in Chapter 1 there has been a wealth of research into the importance of talk for learning (see, for example, Wilkinson, 1968, 1975; Barnes, 1979; Mercer, 1995; Cortazzi, 1997.) Moreover, with Speaking and Listening now constituting a third of the English curriculum (in the National Curriculum of England and Wales), the importance of spoken language is highlighted.

However, despite the rhetoric about the importance of spoken language, the awareness amongst teachers and educators of issues of communication breakdown and repair is not always high. This is illustrated by the following extract from an interview with a former teacher and education officer who is currently researching issues related to exclusion of learners from minority ethnic groups. Despite his substantial educational experience, the research fellow confesses to not having previously considered the 'problem' of breakdown in communication in education:

> I have not thought about this one before. But silence is a problem in the context of western pedagogy because we require oracy in the classroom . . . So it does get in the way of working with students and bringing them out to talk about their involvement in the sort of classroom activities which have come to be typical in

schools . . . So the phenomenon of silence does pose problems to teaching and learning in our classrooms. But it does not . . . it does not pose a behavioural problem. It is not something which gets on teachers' nerves. It is not a behavioural problem which causes teachers distress and which impacts on the rights of other students.

(Collins, 1997)

The speaker in this piece clearly identifies silence as a problem in terms of teaching, learning and assessment. However, his acknowledgement that silence is not a behavioural problem for teachers and other learners might well suggest why, despite his years of experience in education, he has not thought about the issue before. It is practically difficult for teachers to hear and respond to learners' silence in a room full of noise. Quiet learners do not present a discipline problem and consequently their educational, social and emotional needs are not identified and met (Collins, 1996). It has been suggested (for example, ILEA, 1985) that teachers are less alert to signs of emotional difficulty that create problems for the individual pupil than they are to the more overt behaviour that presents them with control or discipline problems.

In trying to maintain channels of communication it is important to recognize that teachers working with quiet learners are faced with a dilemma. Allowing learners to be passive observers deprives them of important learning experiences, but these learners may appear to be so nervous that even the gentlest persuasion seems like a violation. Consequently, it can be difficult for teachers to know how to handle extremely quiet learners even in a one-to-one situation. As one nursery nurse in the above-mentioned study describes, earning the trust of some individuals can be a painfully slow process:

Leora's a very quiet child. She won't approach you, she's a distant child. When she first started nursery, you walked towards her, she used to back off. So she's one that I had to treat in a different way. I used to like her to know that I knew she was there. So with her I had to sort of walk past her but smile and say, hello Leora, but carry on walking. Because she felt threatened if you stopped and talked to her. She, you know, and now she looks at me and now she's . . . she's been here five months and she's got only to the point where she looks at me now and she smiles across the room. You know and I smile at her and tell her, oh Leora, oh you look nice today Leora. I like that dress. We've got to the stage where I just stop quickly and say something to her and then move on. She can't cope with this staying with her at all. Like today I had to twice attempt to talk to her and I went round and she wouldn't talk. She'd put her face in the wall and in the end I left her alone.

(Collins, 1997)

Many young quiet learners experience these kinds of difficulties in talking to their teacher on a one-to-one basis. However, a common theme running through all the quiet learners' accounts of classroom talk in Janet Collins's research is the difficulties they experience in competing for, getting or holding their teacher's attention, particularly during large group discussions. The limitations of whole class discussions are well documented and a number of researchers (for example, Barnes, 1979; Cazden, 1988) have found that learners rarely speak in school except in monosyllables. In schools and other educational contexts it is the teacher who has total control of the material to be learned. This is 'controlling not just negatively, as a traffic policeman does to avoid collisions, but also positively, to enhance the purposes of education' (Cazden, 1988, p. 3). But this aids education as the transmission of knowledge, not education as the transformational process of good learning which we are concerned with in this book.

The practical difficulties of working with large groups of learners lead teachers to adopt teacher-centred teaching styles. Such teaching styles ensure that we as teachers remain in control of the learning situation and can direct discussions in ways which we believe enhance learning. Unfortunately, these teaching styles also significantly reduce the opportunities for learners to speak and, as such, co-construct meanings. Extensive use of teacher-directed talk can lead to breakdown in communication. The staff of the Early Years Unit at Honilands School in the London Borough of Enfield have become increasingly sensitized to this.

Working with Melanie Nind in an action research project they have sought to enhance the communication environment of the unit. With many of the young children having difficulties with speech the staff were keen to take positive action without labelling the children in a deficit model. Classroom observations revealed how much of the talk in the child-centred unit was still adult-directed and adult-dominated. By introducing more small group sessions and child-led show-and-tell sessions this balance is changing.

Wilkinson (1968) suggested that, historically, a transmission model of learning was attractive because it encouraged young learners to be passive recipients of knowledge in order to fit them for their appropriate role in society and, 'had they been encouraged to speak, they might have answered back' (Wilkinson, 1968, p. 125). As discussed in Chapter 1, however, advances in socio-cultural views of learning advocate more learner-centred approaches. Nevertheless, there appears to be a disjunction between rhetoric and practice, with the result that transmission models of learning are still evident in many learning situations.

Learners are quick to pick up and adopt transmission models of learning, particularly when the teacher gives the impression that talking in class is often inappropriate or even forbidden. For example, Rasheeda (in Collins, 1996) thought it inappropriate to initiate conversations with her primary school teacher ''cos he has to work, some work to do and I have some work to do and if you like speak to him a lot, he says just carry on with your work'. She seems unaware of the importance of communication for learning or her right to her teacher's attention when she experiences difficulties. The way in which some learners exclude themselves from the learning relationship is also demonstrated by Diana's comment about what she sees as the teacher's role: 'When I am stuck he has to help me . . . work and everything but most of the time he's . . . he's like talking hisself like doing things on the board and things so you can't really talk to him when he is trying to learning the children'. In this account of transmission teaching, this pupil effectively precludes herself from any participation in the discussion for fear of disturbing the teacher. Moreover, she does not include herself in the group of learners being taught. In this way her exclusion and non-participation are confirmed.

Engagement of learners as active participants in classroom talk implies a move to learner-centred pedagogy, with an increased focus on small group discussions. This involves an important shift of emphasis, as the teacher becomes a facilitator of enquiry rather than custodian and final arbitrator of knowledge. Asking learners to collaborate in small group activities is effectively giving them greater control over their own learning. As learners address the tasks set for them they naturally develop them in their own ways and to meet their own needs. However, when learners are encouraged to ask questions there is a danger that they will raise important, personal and potentially controversial issues. These may be outside the aims and objectives of their teacher. They may even be issues beyond the expertise of the teacher. As teachers in such circumstances we are forced to acknowledge our lack of expertise and any image of ourselves as all-knowing becomes untenable.

The problem of inappropriate pedagogy for effective communication may be one of mismatch. We introduced the concept of mismatched interactions in Chapter 2 with examples of mistiming and misjudging stimuli and responses, particularly with children with disabilities. There is plentiful evidence of caregivers and teachers also making sensitive adaptations, however, though for teachers this is linked with learner numbers being small (Cicogani and Zani, 1992). Flexibility can be enhanced by increasing the range of communication partners in the learning situation, but only if they do not all emulate a teacherly style (Hughes and Westgate, 1997).

Learners are diverse and we as teachers need to be able to move beyond our preferred communication styles to those of our learners. For example, Michaels and Collins (1984) describe white children's use of a 'topic-centred' linear style of discourse which their teacher related to easily. In contrast, the teacher was not able to discern the theme or follow and predict the flow of classroom talk when the black children used their 'topic-associating' style of discourse with implicit links. Such cross-cultural misunderstandings and mismatches are commonplace. Ogilvy et al. (1992)

found a fairly consistent picture of staff in a Scottish multi-ethnic nursery school assuming 'a more controlling style' with Asian children (p. 93). This was linked to problems of mutual understanding leading to a 'breakdown in reciprocal communication, resulting in the adult taking control' (p. 93). Their study highlights the discomfort, also found in studies where disability or deafness is a factor, that makes people avoid communications that might not be understood. Greater confidence in potential for communication repair would help to counter this.

The accumulative effect of inappropriate teaching styles, in which the need for learners actively to engage in learning by adequate language use is largely ignored, may produce a learning climate of silence. In schools where children may be rowdy, teachers learn to shut them up as a method of control and survival. Even young adults who are university undergraduates may be so used to silence that they sit passively even in seminars, unable or unwilling to speak. Teachers, for fear that it will lead to disruption, often discourage interaction between learners. However, Azmitia (1998) showed that peer interaction may boost motivation to learn and may consciously assist or model effective learning, especially if a skilled teacher helps to shape the interaction by, for example, creating challenging problems. Friends, in particular, may give one another the emotional support to persist when problem solving becomes demanding, although teachers may be even more inclined to split up friends for fear of too much off-task talking.

A lack of shared understanding

When talk becomes learner-directed this opens up the possibility for learners to take some control over the style and content of the communication and to begin to set their own agenda. This is essential if learners are to assimilate new information with their existing knowledge and make the learning their own. Giving learners (and their parents) a voice in the classroom is important in the genuine pursuit of shared understanding between learners and teachers. The actual lived experiences of many young learners include domestic and racist violence and drug-related crime, and school should not deny these. One of the parents in Janet Collins's (1996) study is clear on this:

> Crack exists and some of the biggest runners for crack and
> cocaine are eleven and twelve. They are not adults. Another issue
> is child abuse. There is a patronizing way in which we talk to kids
> about child abuse, yet they go home and they get abused at
> home. It's like I've seen teachers talking about racism to Black
> children in a way that makes them laugh. Teachers don't come
> out and talk about these issues as they really are.
>
> (Aberash's stepfather, from Collins, 1996)

Ignoring such issues or dealing with them in a patronizing way is likely to alienate learners and deny them a source of support to deal with potentially traumatic events. Moreover, without a debate of these issues learners have little opportunity to reflect on their lives and envisage alternative ways of being. However, seeking the views of learners and their parents can reveal significant and deeply held differences of opinion between the different communities involved. A lack of shared understanding between teachers and learners can be associated with a breakdown in communication, as the following example from Collins (1996) illustrates.

During a series of open-ended conversations with a group of primary school pupils and their parents, all the participants spoke frankly about their experience of racism in school and in the local community. These exchanges revealed deep tensions between the African–Caribbean, Asian and White communities. They also revealed areas of potential conflict between the values of school and those of the wider community. As members of the African–Caribbean community, Aberash's mother and stepfather were extremely critical of the school because, in their view, it had failed to implement what they saw as an anti-racist policy. They bemoaned the shortage of Black teachers in their daughter's school and believed that continual exposure to White images and value systems led to her Anglicization and a denial of her cultural roots. However, their demand for a more multi-cultural policy in the school was in direct contravention of other parents' wishes. Mandy's mother rejected the local secondary school because of its multi-cultural policy. Rasheeda's mother was unhappy for her daughter to go to a school with a high Asian population 'because Asian children are always causing trouble'. Clearly this comprehensive school had a poor reputation with both Asian and White families in the area. However, Mandy's mother's rejection of multi-cultural education went beyond criticism of a particular school. She objected to being asked to provide money for Eid celebrations in Mandy's primary school:

> I don't think it's right at all. I mean, if they come to live in this country they are supposed to live by our law, by our ways. Because we'd have to do it over there anyway. But I just don't like it. And there's no way I'd give Mandy money to pay for Eid. No way at all. I feel so strongly about it. Once or twice when there has been Eid I've kept Mandy off school. I mean she mixes with Asian children, she plays with them. I don't mind that. I just don't like her being pushed into learning about their ways.
>
> (Mandy's mother, from Collins, 1996)

Clearly the families hold completely different views about multi-cultural education and the provision made by the school, yet none of the parents felt willing or able to discuss their concerns with the staff. Consequently, the teachers' relationships with parents and learners were based on the false premise that they shared common opinions and ideals. Real dialogue with learners, parents and other members of the community was seen as too difficult to attempt.

The issue is further complicated by the fact that schools themselves are faced with a serious dilemma. In transmitting and explicating their sponsoring culture's ways of interpreting the world, schools run the risk of perpetuating, however implicitly, a certain version of the world. This can be alienating for those who do not hold those views. Alternatively, openly challenging the sponsoring culture may mean offending others. As Bruner (1996) argues:

> That is the price of educating the young in societies whose canonical interpretations of the world are multivocal or

ambiguous. But an educational enterprise that fails to take the risks involved becomes stagnant and eventually alienating.

(Bruner, 1996, p. 15)

Social and emotional aspects of learning

Research (for example, Greenhalgh, 1994; Collins, 1996; Johannessen *et al.*, 1997) has highlighted the importance of the social and emotional aspects of learning, even for adult learners on vocational courses who have strong instrumental reasons for learning (Harkin *et al.*, 2001). In a study of non-completion of GNVQs (Harkin, 1998b), it was found that among learners still on the course there was a general satisfaction with the quality of teachers and teaching. In the perceptions of students who had dropped out, however, a major factor was a feeling that they had not been sufficiently supported by teachers. By contrast, teachers and institutions rarely saw this as an issue.

As we have argued, because the very act of learning involves challenging our own prior assumptions this means that all learners feel vulnerable and defensive at some time. In addition, many learners bring externally generated anxieties and vulnerabilities with them to the learning situation. Learners who are trying to deal with serious emotional trauma at home or in their community are unlikely to have the energy and confidence to engage with the risky business of learning.

Young children who feel secure about their relationships within the family are usually able to accept the transition to school without undue anxiety. These children 'have learned to tolerate separation from those who are important to them (attachment figures), secure in the knowledge that reunion will follow' (Barrett and Trevitt, 1991, p. 8). Secure learners appear confident and can relate positively to their teachers and peers. They expect others to respond positively towards them, are able to wait for attention and are not overwhelmed by apparent rejection. Such children are self-reliant and can be observed finding solutions to problems independently or in co-operation with their peers. They show a responsive interest and a lively curiosity in a school environment that is initially unfamiliar to them. However, the connection between confidence and secure attachment is only true for most children. It is possible that for other children outgoing behaviour can be a way of hiding or compensating for their discomfort. Conversely, for some children from unsupportive families, their relationship with their teacher and the predictable routines of classroom life can provide a welcome respite from the unpredictable hostility of the outside world. What is clear is that insecure attachments or insecure bases from which to explore can make learning and communication very difficult.

Anxiety can be a tremendous barrier to participation in classroom communications. Aberash, in Janet Collins's study, talked about shyness being 'normal but you get scared out of your wits'. From the same study, Natasha's mother, Joan, many years after leaving school, recalled how her own acute shyness prevented her from focusing on the content of the lessons being taught:

> I mean, you're just sitting there like uptight all the time because I suppose it's a form of . . . you're so concerned about yourself . . . I mean I have to be honest about it, about what people think about you that you just dread everybody looking at you. And therefore you just go into yourself. You sit in a . . . you know, your whole life's . . . you're planning things. Where are you going to sit. Where you would be seen the least. Honestly, you know . . . and just living in dread of the lessons that you um . . . where you are going to have to take part. So in the end I think I just sat at the window going into little dream worlds of my own.
>
> (Joan, from Collins, 1997)

Because she was anxious about talking in front of large groups of relative strangers Joan excluded herself from the public conversations of the classroom. By remaining quiet and allowing other, more vocal members of the class to dominate discussions, she denied herself valuable learning experiences in which she would gain experience of talking and learning through talking. Many learners who do not communicate freely in learning situations have commented on how anxious they feel about talking in large group or whole class situations. Some have also found it difficult to talk to their teacher in one-to-one situations. Here their anxieties were often related to difficulties in forming relationships with their teachers.

'Key skills' in Communication are now a requirement of many programmes of study for young adults and older learners. Anxiety plays a part again here, particularly in the requirement to give a presentation, which learners typically fear but with emotional support want to have a go and to succeed in.

Difficulty in forming relationships

Joan is aware that her daughter Natasha is habitually quiet in school. The fact that she is less quiet at home with her family suggests that her quietness is related to feelings of insecurity in school and a lack of relationship with her teacher.

> Natasha is very quiet and especially in sort of group situations. Which I felt as well that um, it wasn't all one sided. I felt there maybe was a relationship thing there as well, between teacher and child. I think I felt that Natasha was actually very careful with her work but she won't be hurried. But she definitely is a quiet child in class. I mean, there's no doubt that she is. She's not at home. But she . . . but school's different . . . see it's different isn't it? I mean she's got the . . . she feels secure at home. She can just be herself. You're not that secure, I mean from my own experience when you're in a class of children. Some of them are very extrovert you know.
>
> (Joan, from Collins, 1997)

Natasha avoids all but essential dialogue with her teacher and even then the conversation is perfunctory. A lack of relationship with her teacher prevents her from talking to her even on a one-to-one basis. Joan is concerned that this lack of communication might have a detrimental effect on Natasha's learning:

> Once the children have done their basic work they can go and do whatever they want. And I would say to her, 'Have you been on the computer Natasha?' And she'd say, 'No mummy because . . .' she said 'all the other children go on but I don't get a go because

they've asked the teacher.' But she wouldn't ask the teacher, you
know so she'd never get on the computer hardly.

(Joan, from Collins, 1997)

The need to compete with other, more vocal learners may
contribute to Natasha's reluctance to assert her right to use the
computer. However, the initial reticence some learners show
during small group activities and their seeming reluctance to talk
to teachers during one-to-one conversations suggest there are
other factors involved. Aberash's parents, for example, described
her as 'somebody that's probably got a lot of things inside which
she's trying terribly hard to get out' but 'you have to work hard
to get at who she is'. Little wonder that as teachers we spend less
time over the stilted, one-sided conversations which are the best
that we often achieve with quiet learners, and concentrate on
developing relationships with their more demonstrative peers.
Sadly, this represents something of a self-fulfilling prophecy, as
those who experience most difficulty in communicating with
their teachers have least opportunity to improve through practice. The feeling of being ignored when communication fails is
extremely punishing, as Wilkinson (1975) points out:

> There are various ways it is possible to damage human beings
> psychologically: by annoying them, insulting them, threatening
> them, persecuting them. But often it is far more effective to do
> none of these things: to do nothing to them, to leave them
> entirely alone. So in prison solitary confinement is recognized as a
> severe punishment.

(Wilkinson, 1975, p. 95)

When learners feel anxious in the learning situation and are
unable or unwilling to talk about and deal with their anxieties
there is a sense in which they might become invisible to their
teachers. We need to spend time getting to know all our learners
if we are to ensure that we are not unwittingly subjecting them
to periods of solitary confinement.

In this chapter we have asserted the need for learner-centred
pedagogies; the importance of effective relationships; and the
need to be aware of social and emotional aspects of learning. We

have also acknowledged that giving learners a voice in their own education is fraught with tensions. Dialogue occurs between people who are prepared to meet as equals in a trusting relationship. This is extremely difficult for some individuals whose poor self-image means that they feel threatened and experience difficulties in forming and sustaining relationships. Moreover, inequalities are inherent at all levels of the educational system and even in the most liberal of classrooms learners and teachers do not meet as equals. As good learning is active and interactive, dialogue between and amongst teachers and learners is a crucial part of the process. In the next chapter we address ways in which learners' participation in dialogue and learning can be enhanced.

Chapter 5

Learner Perspectives – Why Start Here?

We are concerned in this book with good learning, which is both active and interactive, and as such requires teachers to understand and engage with learners' perspectives. In England and Wales the Teacher Training Agency (TTA), which is responsible at a national level for the recruitment and training of teachers, recently launched a campaign to recruit more teachers with a slogan 'no one forgets a good teacher'. Commercials for the profession featured famous people recalling their favourite teacher and the message was that teachers make a difference to people's lives. The teachers who are remembered are, of course, those with whom a positive relationship was formed. This campaign could be regarded as showing the concern of the TTA with the learners' perspective – how pupils view teachers.

Could the drive to attract more teachers have been based on the idea that 'no teacher forgets a good pupil'? Commercials could feature teachers recalling the pupils who made them laugh, who taught them a thing or two, who challenged them and rewarded them. Such an approach might appeal to those attracted to the 'cuddly-feel-good' elements of the caring or nurturing professions. A focus on both human relationships and pupils as central to the profession of teaching, however, would detract from the centrality of the teacher and the process of imparting knowledge that governments find more comfortable.

When we described, in Chapter 2, the optimal learning environment of the interactions of early childhood, the presence of a relationship between caregiver and infant was so obvious it almost did not need to be said. It is almost impossible to tease out the relative importance of the liking or love the parent as 'intuitive teacher' has for the infant and the style s/he adopts, or indeed how each affects the other. We do know, however, from studies of Intensive Interaction (Nind and Hewett, 1994; Hewett and Nind, 1998) that adopting a nurturing, facilitative, interactive style has often helped teachers to come to like pupils whom they previously found quite difficult to like or get to know. This may be because the style involves teachers in seeking the learners' perspective; the interactions are not established unless the teacher becomes receptive to the learner's preferences and feedback. In this style, seeking and responding to the learner's perspective operates on a non-verbal level, but involves genuine communication. Time and energy are invested in finding out what the learner wants because it is necessary to engaging them in the learning process.

We maintain that finding out how learners see things, i.e. how they see themselves, the teacher and the learning situation, is fundamental to engaging them as learners. Our concern with teaching as an interactive and emotional process inevitably leads us to a concern with learners themselves, as people with whom we have some kind of relationship. Our reciprocal, transactional model of learning means that having separate chapters in this book on learners and teachers is in some ways anomalous. By separating learners from teachers we run the risk of reducing the complexity of their interconnectedness. In addressing this, each of these chapters has inevitably become about both learners and teachers, but we attempt at least to examine the importance of the perspectives of each in turn.

There are some common mistakes made in thinking about how learners see things and we have been guilty of some of them ourselves at various times. First and not least, it is all too easy to assume that we already know how the learner is thinking and feeling: after all, we have all been learners ourselves. The title of a chapter by Grant (1995), 'Unless I chose to tell you, you wouldn't know', powerfully reminds us that this is not the case. Second, it is also easy to generalize and to think that gaining the insights of one or two learners tells the story for all learners, or at least whole groups of learners, whereas each brings their own unique experiences and way of seeing the world. Third, there is a tendency for much rhetoric on this theme: policy documents tend to espouse the idea of learner involvement, but real commitment and action may be lacking.

Fielding's (1999) portrayal of the difference between the 'effective school' and the 'person-centred school' helps to illustrate the difference between rhetoric and reality in attending to learners and their involvement. The person-centred orientation exemplifies real concern; it 'is about the explicit development of students as agents of their own and each others' educational transformation' (p. 284). In this orientation teachers' questions express an integral concern for and detailed knowledge of students as unique individuals and they are asked in a way that is genuinely attentive rather than a 'disguised form of teacherly assertion' (p. 285). For Fielding real concern with learner involvement involves the 'complex reality of a lived partnership', whereas in rhetorical concern 'their [students'] voice is little more than an assenting punctuation mark in an institutionally constructed sentence' (p. 286).

Superficial listening to learners is commonplace. Bliss *et al.* (1996) introduce the concept of 'pseudo-interaction/bypassing' as a common way of explaining why teachers in their study failed to provide 'scaffolding' (i.e. the support needed until the learners can do it for themselves) for their pupils. The attempts, of teachers they observed, to develop joint activity contained some superficially joint features, but whilst teacher and pupil were both present, they were not really interacting and pupils' contributions were minimized. Pseudo-interaction or bypassing, they argue, might take the form of teachers interpreting or translating pupils' contributions into their own thinking, effectively denying the links with the pupils' own knowledge and understanding. Alternatively, the teacher and pupil might both be talking, but each pursuing a different agenda and line of thinking from the other, never really connecting. Bliss *et al.* (1996) understand the causes of this in terms of the nature of schools as opposed to informal learning environments, problems with the kind of subject knowledge covered and teachers' poor understanding of that subject knowledge.

In this chapter we assert our commitment to learners' genuine involvement as a key aspect of our person/interaction/process-centred vision of teaching and learning at its best. The learner's perspective may be very different from that of the teacher, and engaging with learners may mean engaging with difference. In turn, engaging with difference may mean stimulating our thinking about reaching out to all learners (Ainscow, 1999). This difference may be found in all ages and phases of education, but may be most marked in secondary schooling. In consequence, teachers may have to concede some of their power as they seek, value and work with learners' perspectives.

Keele University gathered the views of over 7000 young people about their attitudes to secondary school in Britain. According to Barber (1994), the findings do not make pretty reading. Here is a flavour of student perceptions:

> There is a general lack of motivation among perhaps 40–50 per cent of all pupils in secondary schools.
>
> 70 per cent of pupils agree that they count the minutes to the end of their lessons.
>
> 30 per cent believe that work is boring.
>
> 30–40 per cent take the view that they would rather not go to school.
>
> Over 50 per cent find that in their school pupils make fun of those who work hard.
>
> About 15 per cent of pupils in their early teens find that other pupils make their lives miserable and slightly more than this are bullied sometimes.

Interestingly, despite these marked adverse views, 88 per cent of pupils are 'usually happy at school'! Perhaps this discrepancy has something to do with the fact that for many in secondary school it is not perceived to be 'cool' to like school or to be seen to be working hard and valuing success. However, there is a need to take learners' views seriously and to explore the factors that lead to statistics like these.

Engaging learners

In the beginning, with infants, we adjust ourselves with abandon, to make ourselves interesting to those infants. As we described in Chapter 2, we readily test out how they want us to be in order to engage with them. We reach across the difference in our experiences of the world and our everyday understandings to make a connection. This is what Melanie Nind sought to do with students with severe learning difficulties in Intensive Inter-action (Nind and Hewett, 1994). Similarly, in her work with quiet learners Janet Collins aimed to connect with learners and enhance their engagement through increased insights into the learners' own perspectives of themselves and school. In the *Communication Styles* project and the *Quali-teach* project (Harkin, 1998a; Harkin *et al.*, 2000), Joe Harkin was involved in similar work with much older learners. Both his projects engaged young adults themselves in expressing their perceptions of learning and teaching. As teachers we are likely to need to reach across all kinds of differences – in gender, ethnicity, culture, class, (dis)ability, age, motivation, emotion – so we may engage with our learners and they may engage with us and with learning.

This concern with making connections with learners' perspectives relates to our view of learning as interactive. We need to start from, and value, what our learners bring if we are to avoid a mismatch. We cannot just assume that our learners will adjust to our objectives, priorities and teaching styles. We need to de-centre and see the world through their eyes, so that we can make the curriculum and the learning experience relevant and meaningful.

Early-years practitioners are clear on this, with well-developed notions of a developmentally appropriate curriculum that should not be formalized but should nurture the child's development and learning (Ball, 1994; Anning, 1998; Early Childhood Forum, 1998). Curriculum guidance for the early years focuses on processes rather than content, with areas of development inter-linked and planned holistically, making use of the social context and the play environment. It is well recognized that 'a curriculum divided into subjects is, potentially, the most alienating form of curriculum for young children because it formalizes experience too soon and, in doing so, makes it distant from the everyday, commonsense knowledge and learning that the young child is familiar with and responsive to' (Blenkin and Kelly, 1993, p. 58).

Also clear on this are those seeking to make further, adult and higher education more inclusive, to widen participation and bring in those who have traditionally been on the outside or margins of education. Preece (2000, p. 6) describes this in terms of a need for a local connection: a coalition between the learner's world and ours (as teachers). Indeed, she sees this as crucial for lifelong learning:

> If learners are to engage with the demands of global changes and their contingent unpredictability, their experiences must first be grounded in familiar locales, where difference is given its own sense of certainty, pace and place.
>
> (Preece, 2000, p. 8)

Stuart and Thomson (1995) and their colleagues share experiences of engaging with difference within adult continuing education. They explain that because 'education differentiates and limits who can be a learner and what and how she or he can learn', all of their learners are 'constructed as "other" to the educational norm' (Stuart and Thomson, 1995, p. 1). This sense of 'otherness' becomes internalized such that:

> these tensions between different ways of knowing, and the difficulties students have in engaging with ideas which do not easily connect to, or make sense of, their own particular social experiences, are part of the process which identifies people who don't 'fit' within the accepted knowledge base as different.
>
> (Stuart and Thomson, p. 7).

bell hooks argues that students' lived experiences should become central to academic material. She uses the term 'engaged pedagogy' to describe teaching and learning where everyone's presence is acknowledged:

> To embrace the performative aspect of teaching we are compelled
> to engage 'audiences', to consider issues of reciprocity. Teachers
> are not performers in the traditional sense of the word in that our
> work is not meant to be a spectacle. Yet it is meant to serve as a
> catalyst that calls everyone to become more and more engaged, to
> become active participants in learning.
>
> (hooks, 1994, p. 11)

We support hooks's claim that by using an 'interactive teaching approach' we can validate the marginalized voice. The presentation by Smith-Livdahl *et al.* (1995) of a collection of stories of 'response-centered' teaching illustrates just how responsiveness to what students feel and express can be empowering. With real listening, giving validity to what is heard, teachers value the experiences and perceptions of students and learn from them.

Research exploring learners' perspectives on what engages them has much to offer to our understanding of, for example, the importance of intrinsic motivation. Stevenson (1990, p. 330) recognized that 'it is the student who decides whether to become engaged in academic work' and so he sought the views of 45 students from US high schools to illuminate this process. Students were asked to give examples of situations where they put in their best effort and where they were so interested that time passed quickly. Their examples showed themselves in active roles, engaging in analytic thinking, inductive reasoning and evaluation, through expository writing, oral discourse and creative tasks. Examples also illustrated how important it was that the topic be intrinsically interesting to them or relevant to real world issues or events or connected to their life outside school. We see the importance to learners of getting the balance right between 'challenge' and 'support', which is one of the themes of *Teaching Young Adults* (Harkin *et al.*, 2000).

When interviewees probed for reasons why a lesson was engaging, for over half the students this was about being able to discuss or contribute their own opinions, to manipulate information or work on a challenging problem. A quarter specifically mentioned their teacher's pedagogy and, in particular, making the class fun with stories, variety and socially interactive game-like activities.

Active participation and interesting pedagogy are what many students are conscious of needing to engage them. Batten's (1989) comparison of teachers' and pupils' perspectives on the positive aspects of classroom experience similarly showed that pupils had much to contribute on good pedagogy. She found considerable agreement between the Scottish comprehensive school pupils and their teachers, the encouragement of pupil participation and use of a variety of activities and approaches being most frequently mentioned as positive aspects of teaching strategy by both.

Cooper and McIntyre (1994) similarly found considerable agreement between pupils and teacher about what constitutes effective teaching and learning experiences. Again, significant features were pupils engaging in deep reflection and experiencing a high degree of enjoyment or involvement and, additionally, pupils accomplishing something, within interaction characterized by co-operation and harmony. Pupils defined effective teaching as enabling them to learn – where they can 'perceive personally meaningful connections between their existing knowledge and new knowledge' (Cooper and McIntyre, 1994, p. 636).

The *Communication Styles* project (Harkin, 1999; Harkin *et al.*, 2001) also found general agreement between teachers and young adult learners (aged 16–20) about what constitutes effective teaching. This involves a balance between 'leadership', shaping the learning experience to meet the needs of learners and offering a suitable level of challenge; combined with 'warmth', providing a suitable climate for learning in which the individual feels valued and safe. The process of allowing learners *with* their teachers to, in bell hook's phrase, 'talk back' is potentially frightening for individual teachers and threatening for institutions. Students have traditionally had to know their place in the scheme of things. They may be running riot in some classes, but at least no one asks them for an honest opinion why.

When they are asked, a number of things become clear: they are perfectly sensible and sensitive in what they have to say;

they know a great deal about effective learning and teaching; and they often display significant differences in perception from teachers and institutions, despite being generally satisfied with provision. Listening to their voices is not nearly as threatening as may be supposed, and it is possible for teachers and learners to engage in genuine dialogue to improve learning and teaching. Enfranchising people, as Europe discovered in the twentieth century, does not bring civilization crashing down – especially, we may add, if the franchise leads to little actual change.

OBESSU (the Organizing Bureau of European School Student Unions) has definite views about the nature of education and, in keeping with the way that learners' voices have been marginalized in Britain, most British teachers and educational researchers will not have heard of it. Again, OBESSU's voice will not rock the foundations of Western civilization but may lead to higher levels of student engagement in education. Comments from the OBESSU that we would want to support include:

Quality education should recognize the importance of social and emotional aspects as well as knowledge and skills;

Evaluation of quality shall be conducted with the participation of all the directly involved actors in school education;

Co-operation between the directly involved actors in school education should aim at mutual understanding and respect for each others' roles and concerns.

Through OBESSU, European school students ask to be heard with respect as active partners in education but, beyond this, they also express wider concerns about the nature of European democracy that may be shared with many older people. In a truly democratic society the views of all should be heard and valued. Everyone should be able to influence the decisions that are made by and on behalf of that society. Education for democracy should ensure that the views of learners are heard and respected both within school and in the wider community. Without these rights learners cannot learn how to be democratic and the notion of a truly democratic society becomes threatened.

OBESSU was one of the contributing partners in the EU Socrates project, *Quali-teach*, which elicited the perceptions of effective teaching of 240 students aged about 17, in six European countries. The views of the students were many and varied but did cluster around exactly the same factors of 'leadership' and 'warmth' as the *Communication Styles* project outlined above. Most importantly, young adult learners wish to be respected by teachers, and given emotional as well as cognitive support to learn. They do expect teachers, for example, to explain clearly; but they also value the friendship of teachers – not as equals or buddies – but as fellow human beings with whom they find mutual regard and shared interests. A few quotations from British students will give a flavour of the balanced views of 'good' teaching of so many students:

> Someone who is able to mix a lesson with letting us learn stuff but at the same time not doing so in a patronizing way . . . you've got to respect them but at the same time they've got to respect you, you've got to be able to talk to them, not necessarily about the subject but outside the lesson . . .
>
> (A-Level student)

> Someone who'll let you be relaxed with, but can make it more enjoyable to learn rather than just standing at the front and writing on the blackboard . . . Treating you as an individual rather than just as a class.
>
> (GNVQ Advanced Health and Social Care student)

> Someone who you can actually learn from . . . and it also comes over not so authoritarian, more as fun . . . not too friendly. Someone who is not so detached from the students.
>
> (GNVQ Advanced Business Studies student)

Mutuality and reciprocity

Hearing the voices of our learners and involving them in practice is about learners' entitlement to participate and our duty to listen and to negotiate. It is not about handing over our responsibility as teachers, but it is about our preparedness for our learners to take power. Kansanen (1999) conceptualizes this as teaching–studying–learning interactions that are not symmetrical, because of teachers' legal responsibilities, power and authority, but democratic.

The *Communication Styles* project (Harkin *et al.*, 1999) showed that learners are acutely aware that they need a balance between teacher leadership, in shaping the learning experience, and teacher 'warmth' or emotional support for learning. Giving students 'responsibility' for their own learning, without either the necessary degree of cognitive or affective support, is a recipe for certain failure.

In France, Felouzis (1994) showed that students on different educational tracks tend to emphasize different things in the relationship with teachers:

- 'academic' students say that they are motivated by interest in the subject and wish teachers to light up the subject in interesting ways;
- 'vocational' students wish to learn but at the same time have greater emotional needs for a mutually respectful and warm relationship with teachers;
- and students who are relatively disaffected from education, who may not have done well so far, tend to prefer a relatively strict, disciplined environment to help them regain lost ground.

What is not clear is the extent to which these different needs are the cause or effect of different educational choices. It is possible, for example, that only highly motivated learners can gain access to academic strands of education, or that those who are disaffected have given up on ideas of mutually respectful and warm relationships with teachers.

Fielding (1999) illustrates how target-setting, within a person-centred orientation, can be reciprocal, supporting students' learning and 'enabling of the teacher's learning too; learning about the student, learning from the student, learning with the student, learning about the process of learning and the teacher's role in it'. In this model target-setting conversations are less dominated by teachers' agendas, less managed by teachers, and more a genuinely joint endeavour.

There has been much said within the social inclusion agenda of governments in Europe, the USA, Australia and New Zealand about drawing people from the margins into mainstream society – normalizing them. We question, however, whether if their perspectives had been valued in the first place, they would have become outsiders or whether they would still be engaged in learning. As Preece (2000, p. 4) powerfully argues, if we valued learners and valued diversity, their involvement would not be at the cost of denying their social/cultural identity. In England and Wales, the Connexions service is currently being set up to help young people who are disaffected from education to become engaged again. Its intentions are laudable – to join up different provision for young people, from social services, education and mentoring, in order to support those in need. It is, however, affection for the disaffected and some of the young people may not have become so had there been more affective education in the first place.

Involving ourselves with learners' perspectives means that the power relations between teachers and learners enter a state of flux, with each, as Stuart and Thompson (1995, p. 26) describe, 'at times unsure of their identity in the engagement'. This is where negotiation, reciprocity and mutuality are central. Both traditional teacher and traditional learner become potential teachers and learners. Learning and teaching becomes about engaging in a shared enterprise. Hart's (1996) story of one learner, Annette, illustrates some of the complexities and tensions involved with this:

> Annette showed herself able not only to take the initiative but to organize a powerful and, in many respects, successful remedial programme for herself, restoring her confidence in her own ability to learn. I am convinced that the opportunity to control her writing was vital to this genuine progress, because no teacher, however expert and sensitive, could have known enough about Annette's needs in relation to the complex conjunction of circumstances in which she found herself to have been able to

predict or propose a strategy so perfectly adapted to Annette's experience and existing resources as that which she devised for herself.

(Hart, 1996, p. 52)

However, Annette's story is also a cautionary one, in that because she did not know that writing was about expressing yourself, in some ways her self-developed strategy was also in some ways also a counter-productive one. Hart reflects that this

> provided a salutory reminder of how easy it is to take our own frames of reference for granted and forget how our curricular intentions will be transformed in practice once they have been filtered through children's own systems of meaning . . . Thus, no matter what our expertise, experience or ideology, in the gap between teachers' intentions and children's responses to classroom learning experiences, there is always potential for new, unanticipated problems to emerge.

(Hart, 1996, p. 53)

Hart concludes that what is needed is not to opt out of giving children power because it is too risky, but to apply a continually vigilant process of critical thinking.

Work in the area of autism provides an interesting example of teachers engaging in a shared enterprise with learners. Historically, teachers have seen themselves, and have been seen by others, as having the valuable insights and skills and the insights and skills of individuals with autism have been seen as deficient or damaged. The availability of a series of 'insider' perspectives on autism (Sinclair, 1992; Williams, 1996) has rocked this position. We are having to consider not just whether we should teach people with autism the 'autistic' or 'non-autistic way', but to remind ourselves about diversity within and across autism, so that we may make connections with learners who see the world quite differently. Powell (2000a, p. 113) argues that 'if a teaching and learning episode in autism doesn't engender mutuality (whether that be of sensation, fun or understanding) then it is not likely to lead to learning that is meaningful, flexible and ultimately generalizable'. In our view, it is the challenge in

finding this mutuality with learners with autism, not the importance of the mutuality itself, that makes autism 'special'.

Powell (2000b, p. 11) cites the insider perspective of Jim
Sinclair as crucial guidance on the importance of seeking and
working with learner perspectives. Sinclair (1992) says:

> But my personhood is intact. My selfhood undamaged. I find
> value and meaning in life, and I have no wish to be cured of
> being myself. Grant me the dignity of meeting me on my own
> terms . . . Recognize that we are equally alien to each other, that
> my ways of being are not merely damaged versions of yours.
> Question your assumptions. Define your terms. Work with me to
> build bridges between us.
>
> (Powell, 2000b, p. 11)

This plea to make the task of making connections a reciprocal
one is certainly powerful. It puts difference in its place as
belonging equally to both teacher and learner, as mutual difference. We return to our point about sharing power but not losing
our sense of our responsibilities as teachers. In the reciprocal and
mutual process of making connections to enable learners to
become engaged, it is our responsibility as teachers to make the
first move and to enable the process to happen.

Cooper and McIntyre (1994) provide a helpful concept of a
continuum from transmission to interactive and then reactive
teaching strategies. Teachers engage with learner perspectives
throughout the interactive–reactive part of the continuum but
the extent to which teachers allow lesson activity to be determined by their perceptions of pupils' states and interests varies.
In purely reactive mode this is their first consideration, whereas
in purely interactive mode, the first consideration is their pre-set
objectives. Cooper and McIntyre stress the importance of teachers being able to move back and forth along this continuum,
adapting in the way they integrate their own and pupil concerns.
From researching both teacher and pupil perspectives on effective learning they conclude that it is the bi-directionality of
influence that is crucial: teachers' ability to influence pupils
depends to a large extent on their willingness to be influenced
by them.

Creating relationships for learning

We have talked about enhancing communication through relationships in Chapter 4, and in this chapter it is important for us to make explicit the connections between seeking and valuing the perspectives of learners and building relationships with them. As Greenhalgh (1994) articulates, empathy is the basis for relationship and through relationship meaning and learning develop. Through our interactions in the context of these relationships our sense of self as a learner or teacher develops.

Bruner (1972) suggested that learning is not necessarily dependent on the teachers' skills, but on the uniqueness of the relationship between the learner and teacher. Our research has shown that by focusing on the quality of the relationship we can enhance the quality of the learning. Preece (2000) too, in the North of England project, found that developing positive relationships was vital to enabling teaching and learning.

In her concern for enhancing opportunities for children with limited literacy, Hart (1996) saw potential in shifting the balance from teacher-initiated activities to those initiated by the pupil. She was interested to find conditions in which children could find their own voice and take control of their learning. She cites Graves's observation that children's marks on the paper say 'I am' and school responses often saying 'no, you aren't'. She stresses the need for children to write about what is personally important for them, bridging the gap between their own relevances and the school curriculum. For teachers to support this process, they need to 'build up "territories of information" about each child, that is, knowledge about the child's cultural and experiential world, activities, expertise and interests outside of school' (Hart, 1996, p. 17). Teachers need meaningful interactions with learners while they are in the process of thinking and writing and in which teachers see themselves as learning too.

Active learning

We have articulated in earlier chapters our view of learning as an active process, in which learners are active constructors of knowledge rather than passive recipients of it. As Fielding (1999, p. 286) argues, a view of active learners at the centre of education 'moves beyond students as interesting sources of data, as objects of teachers' professional gaze, to students as co-constructors of new meanings and shared understandings rooted in the unpredictability of dialogue'. If we hold that learners construct their understanding of the curriculum out of their own real experiences, which are constructed to become their own unique reality, we have to find ways to engage with this reality. We need to attend not to either learner *or* content, but to the content as it is being learned by the learner, or to the learner as he or she is learning the content.

This view of active learning is what led Nind and her colleagues to the acceptance of early interactive experiences as being essential for learners at the earliest stages of social and communication development (Nind and Hewett, 1994). It was pointless to offer models of the social world constructed by others: we had to offer experiences that would enable the students to construct this meaning for themselves. Similarly, Joe Harkin's *Communication Styles* work seeks to give both teachers and learners a shared vocabulary to discuss classroom communication in ways that are non-confrontational. It is a paradox that teachers, who are professional communicators, and learners, who participate in education for the notorious 15,000 hours, may be left speechless and unable to begin to talk about how they routinely interact. By contrast, non-routine or confrontational interaction can be talked about readily. Were teachers and learners able to spend time together talking about learning and teaching issues in non-confrontational ways, then many confrontational episodes could be avoided. A belief that learning is, by definition, active led to Janet Collins's concern for and work with pupils who were unable or unwilling to participate in the social and academic discussions of her classroom. These pupils' involvement in pupil-directed small group activities and discussions encouraged them to set their own agendas and to make the learning their own. Within the same research, semi-structured interviews with pupils, their parents and teachers provided participants some scope to construct the world in their own terms.

Similarly, in work with adult learners who did not readily recognize themselves as learners, Preece (2000, p. 10) comments:

> In devising a culturally or socially relevant curriculum . . . the trick was to build on people's lived experiences as a knowledge base to construct new ways of seeing the world.

By building on people's lived experiences we can challenge, with learners, their ideas that 'education is for other people' (Stuart and Thomson, 1995, p. 1). As Stuart (1995a, p. 161) argues, the frequently heard comment amongst mature students that 'I've never done anything with my life' voices 'a social perception of who owns and therefore defines knowledge'. She questions the ability of accreditation of prior experience/learning (APEL) to do other than endorse the structural inequalities that mean people have unequal access to experiences. In contrast, *recognition* of prior experience/learning, she believes, can do much more. Stuart (1995a, p. 166) explains how a 'life history approach' to recognizing prior learning 'allows individuals to shape and explore their own experiences within their own choice of narrative'. In this kind of approach, just as in Intensive Interaction or Harkin's Communication Styles work or work with quiet learners, teachers really have to engage with learners' different experiences.

Adult liberal education has traditionally taken into account the particular learning needs of adults and offered opportunities 'to contest traditional assumptions about pedagogy and what constitutes knowledge' (Holloway, 1995, p. 142). Holloway explains this in terms of Crombie's contextualist epistemology in which the individual's experience is central learning point:

> It is the 'learner-in-the-world', the experiences, challenges, problems, mysteries and so on that motivate curiosity and enquiry. In practice, this means moving alongside the learner, entering the learner's world, in order to be able to guide and support the further exploration of reality.
>
> (Holloway, 1995, p. 145)

In summary, education involves valuing and entering the learners' world and empowers learners to become active participants. This happened with the profoundly disabled young people in Intensive Interaction (Knott, 1998; Smith, 1998). It also happened in Bellis and Awar's (1995) bilingual ESOL class:

> When we placed equal value on the learner's language, there was a change in the dynamics of classroom interaction: the learners became more active and assertive; everyone had the opportunity to participate and there were far more interruptions, questions, 'asides' and digressions.
>
> (Bellis and Awar, 1995, p. 33)

We are conscious, in this book, that in our learner-centredness, we do not neglect the significance of wider social influences and power dimensions. For Foucault (1980), power and knowledge are correlative. They are found together in 'regimes of truth'. As such, he argues, learning and knowledge are both empowering, by generating active students, better able to understand themselves and the world, but also better able to control, as regimes of knowledge limit and prescribe that understanding.

Learner power can be given, but it can also be taken. Davies's (1984) analysis of 'pupil power' shows how students can use deviant scripts to re-assert power over an institution that has denied them dignity. Power is about an ability to influence others. We need to recognize education's power to silence and to empower. In the experience of Janet Collins (1996), this involves considering: the relevance of the curriculum on offer, the appropriateness of the chosen teaching styles, the quality of the relationships which exist within and outside the classroom, as well as a genuine willingness to understand and value the lived experiences of others.

Many learners lack power and lack recognition that their knowledge or experience is valued. This is especially true where, for a number of reasons, which may be related to class, race, gender, perceived ability, etc., the experiences, values, ideals and expectations of those in school differ markedly from those in the wider society.

Individuals in the special education sector, for instance, have until recently been seen as unworthy of having their perspectives heard. They have been done to, rather than engaged with. This has meant they have been denied a role as active learners. Lack of action has meant lack of impact and in turn a limited sense of agency resulting in 'learned helplessness' (Seligman, 1975). McGee *et al.* (1987) called for a posture of solidarity with such marginalized learners, expressed by human warmth, and with pedagogy focused on mutual change – 'gentle teaching'. Interactive approaches, in which teacher responsiveness has been the key to hearing and working with learners' perspectives, have helped to reverse this group's lack of power to influence their teachers (Nind, 2000). Many believe similar work is needed to empower students, including vocational education. For example, it is currently clear, to students as well as to others, that vocational education is regarded as being of lower status than 'academic' education. OBESSU, for example, recognizes that

> in many countries, Vocational Education and Training is considered to be of lower status in society than general secondary education. We wish to find some solutions on how vocational education can become a qualitative equally good alternative to general secondary education, offering interesting opportunities for young people.
>
> (OBESSU, 1996)

In this chapter we have focused on learner perspectives and in the next we turn to teacher perspectives. We acknowledge the interrelationship between these and the need to consider them in tandem.

Chapter 6

Do Teachers' Perspectives Matter?

We have talked a lot in the previous chapter about the need for teachers to be open to learners' perspectives. In this chapter we emphasize the importance of teachers also being open to curricular and pedagogic change: recognizing the principles outlined in this book, and thus facilitating good learning, may mean starting afresh or even rejecting our own or others' common practice. A central theme in this chapter is the way in which we, as teachers, regard our learners, the learning process and our teaching. These perceptions are at the heart of our practice. In keeping with Sergiovanni and Starrat's (1988) model of culture as like as onion, with a belief and value system at the heart and patterns of behaviour as the outer skin, we believe that by thinking about our work differently, we can practise differently. This is why this is an ideas book, of vision rather than recipes for action, for it is our understanding that once the thinking is right, the activity follows. Great effort may need to be put into skill development; but equally, competence may evolve from the mindset. Within this model, we are not envisaging the worst case scenario described by Day (2000, p. 102) in which 'teaching will be just a job' and teachers will be 'technically proficient . . . if without vision'. In contrast we endorse his recognition of the central part teachers have to play in nurturing a love of learning in all learners.

Carrington (1999) distinguishes between teachers' *espoused theory* – what they say they value and intend – and teachers' *theory in use* – the beliefs and intents that can be inferred from their behaviour. We use examples from our own work and that of others, across a range of education phases, to show that espoused theories and theories in use may become more congruent, because of a process of critical reflection, based partly on allowing learners to 'talk back', so that their perspectives are taken into account. These are also positive illustrations of behaviour following mindset and of our regard for teachers as whole people, for, as Day (2000, p. 108) sums up, 'it is the teachers' whole self that brings significance to the meaning of the teaching act'.

Teaching, like learning, is an emotional experience and Nias (1996) in asserting this emphasizes that she does not mean that emotion is split from cognition. 'The emotions are rooted in cognition' and 'one cannot separate feeling from perception, affectivity from judgement' (p. 294). Nias points out that teachers' feelings have received scant academic attention and that, because they are such an important element in their professional work, this is a grave deficit. Teachers have a deep emotional investment in their work because they work in intensive interactions with many individuals each day. Moreover, they are held responsible for the quality of this interaction. The collection of essays in Nias's account show a wide range of teacher emotion, from passionate caring about subjects and students to abject despair at OFSTED inspections and the brutality of intruder judgements.

We argue in this book that it is desirable to open non-confrontational dialogue between teachers and learners about the nature of education and the process of teaching and learning. It is easy to judge people – teachers are constrained to judge learners, and learners, in less formal ways, judge teachers. Teachers are also routinely, and often harshly, judged by parents, managers and inspectors. Teaching is a highly complex and challenging activity and, just as learners need the support of teachers, so too teachers need support, from parents, managers, governors and others. Importantly, however, support – whether by teachers for learners or of teachers by others – cannot become complacency. We have seen in earlier chapters how disaffected from education many young people are. This is not necessarily the fault of teachers, for there are many and complex reasons for this disaffection. However, quite clearly teachers face most directly the consequences of this disaffection. Teachers must be supported critically to reflect on their practices, even in a culture of education that tends increasingly to treat them as technicians, there to transmit information and to judge pre-determined outcomes.

We will begin by looking at some examples of teachers attempting this difficult process of critical reflection on practice.

Teachers developing Intensive Interaction

We have made reference throughout this book to the approach of Intensive Interaction as an example of learners, with very severe difficulties with learning, being enabled to become active learners in mutually enjoyable, reciprocal interactions. The approach is based on principles from early caregiver–infant interaction and illustrates the fact that human relating is funda-mental to effective teaching and learning. It also shows how teachers' perspectives are the central cog in the wheel that made being able to relate to each other happen. Nind and Hewett (1994) describe some of the teachers' early thought processes:

> There was growing unease with a curriculum which seemed to produce regular failure for both the teacher and the student. There was growing discomfort also with the inflexibility of a curriculum structure which gave little scope for following up the students' interests and strengths. To summarize what was in fact a gradual and untidy process, we as a teaching staff began to question both the ethics and the effectiveness of the methods we were using. We began to recognize that much of the behaviour of our students was a response to situations that they did not understand and that they were often demonstrating communication difficulties rather than behaviour difficulties. This led us to look afresh at the students and their fundamental learning needs.
>
> We came to the conclusion that these [fundamental learning] needs were almost always within the realm of communication and sociability and that the existing curriculum rarely even touched upon addressing such needs. We felt that if we could establish a

relationship with the students, and if we could establish a basis for communication, then all other spheres of teaching and learning would become easier and more meaningful . . . With the realization that there were no readily available answers about how to teach the earliest stages of communication and being social to young people with such learning difficulties, we began to seek a new teaching practice for ourselves. We entered a period in which practical experimentation in the classroom and theoretical inquiry complemented and informed each other, and from which new ways of working evolved.

(Nind and Hewett, 1994, pp. 5–6)

You will note that seeing things from the students' perspective was integral to these teachers thinking critically about their practice. Questioning practice began from 'hearing' the students' communication that the curriculum was not meaningful for them. Awareness of how to move forward was greatly helped by the pointer (from psychologist, Ephraim, 1979) to early interaction in parenting as a model for how early communication and social abilities could be fostered. What followed illustrates that whether the direction of one's thinking is going to be productive can be self-evident:

In our practice at school we began to incorporate interactive play into our daily routines . . . Such changes in approach were immediately rewarding, both because the students responded positively and because our work in itself became more enjoyable . . . There followed a spiralling effect of positive change. Gentler, more playful work with individual students was found to be more enjoyable and effective and so was generalized to work with other students . . . Gradually this kind of activity moved from the periphery of the school curriculum to its core.

(Nind and Hewett, 1994, pp. 6–7)

From stopping and asking 'What are we doing here?' there emerged new ways of thinking, and from new ways of thinking emerged new practice. Some of the new practice was consciously linked to new perspectives, but not all. Nind and Hewett (1994, p. 7) recount that 'without at first realizing it we stopped dominating the classroom with our rules and choice of activity and began to be responsive in a very basic kind of negotiation'. The conscious choice was in 'allowing ourselves to use our natural teaching styles' and the spillover was vast. Even the way in which the day and physical environment were organized was not untouched by a new mindset and style of interaction. Aware of the need for accountability and the benefits of reflection, the staff group sought to match the written curriculum with changed practice and, by describing it, to further understand that practice. Those of us involved with this project were acutely aware of teaching as an interpersonal activity, of the importance of what Day (2000, p. 108) calls 'interactive chemistry' between learners and teachers, and of teaching as an expression of personal values.

Collaborative problem-solving

Intensive Interaction is currently being used by one English education authority as a vehicle for supporting teachers thinking about the dynamics that create difficulty with learning. The policy-makers are concerned with inclusion and they are trying to move local thinking towards a social model of disability, locating difficulties within contexts rather than individuals (Nind and Cochrane, in press). This is being pursued within a problem-solving framework and the empowering, social constructivist orientation of interactive approaches is seen as offering a positive way forward. Funds are not being used to send the most challenging pupils to specialist placements outside of the local area, but rather to support opportunities for 'praxis'. Melanie Nind is acting as a resource for this, like a critical friend in the action research model, asking challenging questions and being a sounding board for ideas.

Pupils who are usually defined by the nature of their deficits are being reconceptualized as pupils who fall outside of the routine competence and confidence of teachers (in mainstream and special schools). Neither teacher nor pupil is blamed for difficulties that are experienced with teaching and learning, but the emphasis is on problem-solving around the pedagogic dynamic. The project aims to extend teachers' competence and confidence and to extend the diversity of pupils that they feel they can confidently respond to with appropriate teaching strategies and curricula.

The project was launched with a challenge posed to the educational community to explore the potential of practitioners from a group of schools working together on a shared problem. The story and principles of Intensive Interaction were presented, and practitioners were encouraged to reflect on the following: Where does existing practice already fit with the principles? Which aspects of practice might they re-think and develop? What do they want to achieve? What support might they need? How might they enable each other and how they might evaluate their action?

The project's focus on 'pupils falling outside of the routine competence and confidence' of teachers clearly reflected a very real agenda amongst many of those involved (Nind and Cochrane, in press). The teachers spoke of their lack of confidence with considerable honesty, but this was accompanied by a strong desire to label the pupils who were challenging them. Initially there was a strong temptation to reject the policy-makers' re-conceptualization of the pupils, and to use instead categorical labels to signify that the pupils belonged elsewhere, in a different category of provision, with a separate breed of teachers who had the specialist skills required. There was a very strong feeling of *our* pupils and *intruder* pupils and whilst there was recognition that the *intruders* were part of the schools' future, and their needs would have to have to be addressed, initially the teachers were willing to do this is only on an add-on basis. They were less ready at first to re-think their whole curriculum offer and approach.

Reflecting on interactive approaches enabled us as a problem-solving community to focus attention on the match between what the pupil brings and needs and what the learning situation offers. Familiarity with Intensive Interaction led us towards looking for answers to the challenge presented by particular pupils in the process of observation, feedback and reflection on the interaction process. A focus on classroom processes and dynamics has been a catalyst for teachers' thinking and exploration to find a curriculum framework flexible enough to be meaningful for a great diversity of learners. The project has involved us in looking at how our practice is interwoven with our personal histories and with an investment in learning partnerships and teams.

How does changing thinking change practice?

Janet Collins's ongoing teaching (e.g. Open University, 2001) and research (e.g. Collins, 2000a) also highlight the need to establish a match between what the learners bring and what the learning situation can offer and the way in which changing thinking changes practice. Her focus on the educational, social and emotional needs of quiet pupils began as she reflected with colleagues on transcripts of classroom discussion (Collins, 1993). These discussions appeared to exclude a number of the primary-aged children who had been present but who had not spoken and who did not appear to have followed the discussion of others. Based on a fundamental belief that learning involved active participation, Janet Collins's initial concern was to work with these quiet learners and to increase their participation in class discussions (Collins, 1994; 1996). The aim was not to create a dramatic change in behaviour such that these children would become the most vocal children in the class. Rather, the aim was to encourage these children to exhibit a range of behaviours and to work towards a situation in which they were able and willing to contribute to some class discussions and to be seen to take a more active role in practical learning activities. Thus the initial focus was the behaviour of the learners and the difficulties they might be experiencing in terms of talking in class.

A commitment to understanding the pupils' perceptions of the learning experience and a willingness to provide them with a relatively safe environment in which to work led to the setting up of small withdrawal groups. Working with pupils outside the mainstream classroom for an hour a week provided them with an opportunity to participate in discussions within a small group context. Working in a small group also provided easier opportunities for them to reflect on the dynamics of group discussions and to try out different roles and strategies. The pupils' comments about these withdrawal groups suggested that they found them helpful and supportive. Moreover, there was clear evidence of increased and sustained participation in the group discussions. These changes in pupil behaviour continued during the following year, as Janet Collins began to work with these pupils alongside their peers in whole class situations.

Interestingly, a close analysis of the discussions that took place in small groups and in the whole class revealed that a change in the pupils' behaviour was reflected in a change in Janet's teaching style. She believes that this is related to a number of factors, including a change in the quality of the relationships between participants, an increased awareness of the experiences and needs of these particular learners and a willingness to adapt the curriculum and pedagogy to help meet those needs. As these ideas permeate the book and inform much of our thinking on education it is worth looking at Janet Collins's experience in a little more detail.

Before embarking on the research, Janet hypothesized that the quality of relationships between teachers and learners and amongst peers was likely to be a contributing factor in some learners' inability or unwillingness to participate in class discussions. Indeed, in early interviews the pupils reported that they felt acute anxiety about appearing foolish in front of teachers and peers. The same interviews also identified a lack of warm trusting relationships between these learners and others in the school. As a consequence, the personal, health and social education (PHSE) curriculum was adapted and a discussion of friendships and other relationships became a focus for the small group discussions. However, perhaps more significant were the changes in the quality of the relationships between Janet and the pupils involved. During the three-year research project Janet observed the pupils in a number of classrooms, working with a range of teachers. She had also interviewed the pupils and their parents on a number of occasions and even visited some of them at home. As a consequence of this extended contact, Janet, the pupils and their families came to know each other much better than is normally the case between primary teachers and pupils. Knowing something about their out-of-school experiences certainly helped Janet to see them as whole people and to understand more of what made them behave in the way they did. Learning about each other in a small group situation, the pupils became more relaxed in each other's company and thus became more able to take risks and share views and opinions. As one of the pupils said, 'No. I'm not shy at home . . . 'cos I know people . . . I know all the people at home . . . don't know all the people at school.' For these learners, knowing the people in school was an important prerequisite for participation in the social and emotional discourse of the classroom.

Participation in the research changed Janet's relationships with the learners. It also changed her understanding of the experiences and needs of these particular learners and led to an adaptation of both the curriculum and pedagogy. Working with these quiet learners over a prolonged period of time provided some insights into their perceptions of themselves and the learning situation. As a direct consequence of these insights, Janet changed her teaching style and placed much more emphasis on small group discussions amongst self-selected 'talk partners'. Understanding some of the difficulties which young learners experience in initiating and sustaining discussions of school-based work in the classroom, Janet began to establish and make explicit with the pupils some of the ground rules of effective talk in school. As part of this process the pupils were asked to reflect on and evaluate their participation in discussions as well as occasionally commenting on the participation of others. For the first time in her teaching career, effective pupil-directed small group activities and discussion became an integral aspect of teaching and learning in Janet's classroom. What she has learned in terms of establishing a match between the learning situation and pupil needs continues to influence her research with other teachers (e.g. Collins *et al.*, 1995, Collins and Syred-Paul, 1997; Collins and Marshall, 2001) as well as her teaching in higher education.

Reflection and action on communication style

As teachers we are professional communicators – and yet, just as little in our training and development prepares us for the emotional challenges of teaching, little prepares us for our role as communicators. It is rare for teachers to have feedback about their styles of interacting with learners, except, on rare occasions, as part of sometimes threatening inspections or appraisals. Routine discussion between teachers and learners about how they tend to work together is rare for several reasons. First of all, both teachers and learners may not share a vocabulary adequate to the task. Second and understandably, teachers may fear losing control over the process of interaction. Third, there is no tradition of learners being consulted in this way, and indeed some schools and colleges may even frown on it. Finally, as we have seen, teaching is an intensely emotional activity, and it is a brave teacher who lets learners comment freely about the process, because of the potential loss of face if they are critical. Thus there are formidable obstacles to teachers' and learners' sharing of understandings and perceptions about interaction in learning. And yet learning is always and everywhere about interaction.

Joe Harkin became more acutely aware of this dilemma when working with teachers on the development of key skills in Communication. If learners are genuinely to be given opportunities to develop their skills in Communication, then very often teaching and learning processes will have to change. Highly didactic forms of teaching, which grant learners only passive roles in formal learning – as distinct from informal and off-task activity – are not capable of enriching the students' use of language. How, though, can any teacher begin exploring how they tend routinely to interact with learners, except by engaging with the learners' perspective – uncomfortable as this may be?

The *Communication Styles* project (Harkin *et al.*, 1999; Harkin *et al.*, 2001) was an attempt to help teachers and learners engage in such an exploration, in a process of self-directed professional development. Chapter 9 explains the project in more detail but here we will say something about the process of teachers becoming engaged in the research. Over one hundred teachers, from eight different schools and colleges, took part in the project at various times by completing a Communication Styles questionnaire and, most challengingly, having their students complete the questionnaire too. In this way, the perceptions of both teacher and learners were unveiled and the items on the questionnaire gave all participants a vocabulary with which to discuss the results. The researchers then facilitated discussion, first of all with the teacher–researcher exploring his or her own perceptions of work with a group of learners, and then, in most cases, between all parties, including the students.

The student voice in these discussions was always polite, well balanced and insightful. If given an opportunity to be taken seriously, these young adults (most of whom were aged about 16–20) talked and listened using the normal conventions of adult-to-adult interaction. This was despite the fact that they were taking the full range of courses post-16, and some of them had been labelled as having educational or behavioural difficulties. For each teacher who participated, there were different aspects of teaching and learning upon which to reflect. There were distinct patterns in both teacher and student views, and a great deal of fundamental agreement about the characteristics of good teaching.

Good teaching, in the perceptions of both teachers and students, is a balance of two sets of professional behaviours – 'leadership' and 'warmth'. These terms are explained more fully in Chapter 9. Both factors are essential in an holistic way. Leadership carries with it elements of warmth, in contradistinction to authoritarianism, which is also a form of control, but is exerted without positive regard. Warmth carries a large element of leadership because if you really care about the welfare and development of students, you will shape the learning experience to meet their needs. Leadership translates into the setting of high standards, both for yourself and the learners; warmth translates into understanding the students and giving them opportunities to become independent learners. This is enacted in a similar way to caregiver behaviour in which infants are encouraged to become independent but in ways that are safe and structured. They are not simply thrown into independence.

Clearly there are formidable practical difficulties in teachers' working with learners in ways they regard as ideal. These will vary between teachers but include extrinsic factors, such as timetabling and curriculum and assessment issues, as well as transactional factors, such as the willingness of learners to work in different ways. Both teachers and learners may have become habituated to ways of working that are not ideal for learning but habits acquired over years are hard to break. In consequence, although all teachers said that they had learned a lot from using the Communication Styles questionnaire, and many teachers found that it improved their relationship with learners and the classroom climate, few in practice were able to use the results to actually change their teaching. A number of factors are involved here, including a perception that the teachers feel they are too busy to change.

Just as many people say that they must take more exercise but rarely get around to it, so teachers are caught up in wishing to change but being unable to find the time or energy for this. In part, at the time of the research in the late 1990s, they were too busy constantly changing in response to government initiatives to allow time for consideration of developing their pedagogy. There is then an irony for teachers. The essence of their teaching – the communication with learners – is something that is a luxury to even reflect on systematically and something very difficult to develop, except organically, over time, as they mature as persons and teachers. Unfortunately, such organic growth may or may not develop better ways of working with learners. Albert Camus said that people change only in novels. This is a thought that challenges all our attempts at action research and self-directed professional development.

It may be necessary for whole institutions to take such reflection, including student voice, as the starting point for collegial development and the growth of genuine learning communities.

Teachers' innovative thinking

Moving beyond our own work, in Hart's (1996) *Beyond Special Needs*, we see how Hart's thinking developed as a result of studying the learning processes of two pupils in mainstream secondary schools. It was, however, her readiness to learn in this way that enabled the exciting innovative thinking described in her book to develop. From the opening pages we see that Hart herself is acutely aware of the potential of mindset for enabling or stifling development:

> I have called the book *Beyond Special Needs* because I believe that in order to open up new possibilities we can and should now set aside once and for all the language of 'learning difficulties' and 'special needs'. This language shapes and constrains our thinking, limiting our sense of the scope available to us for positive intervention to a narrowly circumscribed set of possibilities. It has discouraged mainstream teachers from using their knowledge, expertise and experience as fully and powerfully as they might in pursuing concerns about children's learning.
>
> (Hart, 1996, p. x)

Hart rejects the idea of individualizing concerns about children's learning and disconnecting them from school processes and illustrates how alternative thinking can 'restore mainstream teachers' belief in their own power to take positive action' (p. x). She explains that her approach is 'not conditional upon the availability of additional support or resources ... nor does it expect teachers to possess superhuman capacities or assume an exhaustive knowledge of literature and research' (p. x) and that:

> What the approach does depend upon is a spirit of open-mindedness and willingness to entertain alternative possibilities. It depends upon the conviction that the picture we currently have of children's characteristics as people, and their abilities as learners, is susceptible to change; indeed, that we have the power and means to bring about changes ourselves by thinking in ways that continually open up new possibilities. I call this 'innovative thinking'.
>
> (Hart, 1996, pp. x–xi)

There is already a pattern emerging with Intensive Interaction and innovative thinking in which teachers' sense of themselves as powerful, as having potential as agents of change, is critical. Intensive Interaction evolved in England prior to the National Curriculum when teachers had relative freedom to shape curriculum content. Nonetheless, the teachers questioned and challenged the status quo of the behavourial thinking of the day. There will always be factors that work to constrain our practice, but we contend that it is our relationship with those factors that enhance or reduce their power as constraints.

Hart (1996, p. 102) provides a framework of five questioning moves, which 'help us to move beyond what we already think and know about the situation by probing what has not so far been examined within our existing thinking about the situation', thus 'questioning existing interpretations from a variety of perspectives'. The moves Hart is recommending in this framework are:

- teachers *making connections* between learners' responses and the context in which they occur;
- *contradicting*, teasing out and re-evaluating the assumptions underlying our understanding of the situation;
- *taking the child's eye view* to find the meaning and purpose for the learner;
- *noting the impact of feelings* about the situation on our interpretation of it; and
- *suspending judgement* while we review our interpretation and resources to act.

Again teachers' and learners' perspectives become intermingled and transactional in this model. Like Hart, we are concerned with engendering in teachers a sense of their own power and a sense of using this responsibly. We return to Hart's innovative thinking when we look at co-operative and collaborative learning in the next chapter.

Social constructivist thinking

In Chapter 1 we outlined our own social constructivism, stressing the interactive nature of learning and the importance of language and communication. Watson (2000) argues that such social constructivist perspectives in teachers lead to practice that promotes, amongst other advantages, learners being active, teachers being responsive and social experiences being integral to learning and being valued. As we do here, she reflects on a range of examples of good teaching and learning, and for her the connection is teachers' commitment to social constructivist theory and practice.

Watson explains that the chances that learners will have 'breakthroughs' or 'episodes of intellectual challenge', when they are 'engaged, their attention held and their interest made clear through their words and behaviours' (p. 137), depend on their teachers' perspectives and interactive style. Teachers who are social constructivists give learners the opportunity to forge connections, to manipulate information in ways they find personally meaningful, to work together to negotiate meaning.

Day (2000) reminds us that the visions we hold, of how teachers and teaching should be, are also socially constructed. As such we need to maintain or develop these visions and not take them for granted as abstract and separate. The next example shows the vision of the teacher in question in the making.

Teaching to transgress

bell hooks (1994), working in American higher education is, like Susan Hart, very much aware of teachers' power – to dominate or to liberate. She makes explicit links between how teachers see their role, how they enact their teaching and how learners come to see learning. She recollects her early education in the 'apartheid South':

> Almost all our teachers at Booker T. Washington were black women. They were committed to nurturing intellect so that we

could become scholars, thinkers and cultural workers – black folks who used our 'minds'. We learned early that our devotion to learning, to a life of the mind, was a counter-hegemonic act, a fundamental way to resist every strategy of white racist colonization. Though they did not define or articulate these practices in theoretical terms, my teachers were enacting a revolutionary pedagogy of resistance that was profoundly anti-colonial.

(hooks, 1994, p. 2)

She explains that these teachers were on a mission and to fulfil that mission they 'made sure they knew us . . . our parents, our economic status, where we worshipped, what our homes were like, and how we were treated in the family' (hooks, 1994, p. 3). In this way learning was contextualized and joyful for hooks. Her teachers made school for her at this time a place of pure pleasure, edged with danger. In contrast she describes her later racially integrated schooling:

Gone was the messianic zeal to transform our minds and beings that had characterized teachers and their pedagogical practices in our all-black schools. Knowledge was suddenly about information only. It had no relation to how one lived, behaved. Bussed to white schools, we soon learned that obedience, and not a zealous will to learn was what was expected of us.

(hooks, 1994, p. 3)

The interaction between the teachers' perspectives and the learners' experience are transparent here. hooks goes on to make transparent too the relationship between this interaction and how she developed and saw herself as a teacher. She learned the difference between 'education as the practice of freedom and education that merely strives to reinforce domination' (p. 4) and learned about the kind of teacher she wanted to become:

When I entered my first undergraduate classroom to teach, I relied on the example of those inspired black women teachers in my grade school, on Friere's work, and on feminist thinking about radical pedagogy. I longed passionately to teach differently from the way I had been taught since high school. The first paradigm that shaped my pedagogy was the idea that the classroom should be an exciting place, never boring.

(hooks, 1994, p. 7)

hooks' engaged pedagogy (introduced in Chapter 5) crosses accepted boundaries in many ways; seeking excitement in her sector of higher education runs counter to the seriousness that is assumed to be needed. Her approach necessitates, she argues, a flexible agenda, spontaneity, interaction and critical reflection. The similarity with the description of excitement in Intensive Interaction (and, with the exception of critical reflection, intuitive infant pedagogy) is striking. hooks also argues that engaged pedagogy must acknowledge everyone's presence in a classroom dynamic in which everyone contributes and 'excitement is generated by collective effort' (p. 8). Again there is real resonance here with earlier chapters in this book, and particularly with the contrasting picture of barriers to communication portrayed in Chapter 4.

hooks is convinced that in the process of teaching to empower students, teachers have to be 'actively committed to a process of self-actualization that promotes their own well-being' (p. 15). The interaction should enrich and enhance both learners and teachers. Teachers, like students, need to be open, need to take risks, if they too are to grow and to be empowered by the process.

Perspectives developing as process

We have used a series of detailed examples to explain our view that teachers' and not just learners' perspectives are critical. Teachers' perspectives have much to contribute to an understanding of the concept of rich teaching and learning we advocate in this book. Many teachers engaged in research and development projects such as those outlined here have taken opportunities to reflect on their action so that they may at least attempt to bring their practice into line with their beliefs. Their perspectives are developed and developing as part of a reflective process and a 'mutually illuminating interplay' (hooks, 1994, p. 10) of different pedagogies and influences.

It is this process itself, as much as the particular perspectives that we have included, that we want to engender. As Ainscow (1999) reflects, teachers know more than they use and the important task is not giving new knowledge, but helping and supporting teachers to reflect on their own perspectives and practice. This needs to happen in context so that learning can be personalized and meaningful. Concerned, as are we, with movement towards more inclusive practice, Ainscow (1999, p. 11) argues that this 'comes not from making marginalized adjustments, but rather asking fundamental questions'. We need to take risks and we are more secure in doing this if we reflect on our values and our practice and where these come from. We need to be able to critically question our cultural assumptions, perhaps reconsidering our thinking by 'making what is strange familiar and what is familiar strange' (Ainscow, 1999, p. 2). We need to engage with our own and 'other' perspectives so that we do not just reproduce discriminatory thinking and practice.

Teachers' perspectives and emotions

We have talked of learners and their social and emotional needs as learners and as people. We have illustrated the power of teachers as fellow humans to meet those needs and harness potential. We want to stress also the social, emotional and human needs of teachers and teaching. Hargreaves (1998) portrays this at its most positive:

> Good teachers are not just well oiled machines. They are emotional, passionate beings who connect with their students and fill their work and their classes with pleasure, creativity, challenge and joy.
>
> (Hargreaves, 1998, p. 835)

He acknowledges, however, that the reality of teachers' emotional lives may be less rosy and argues that we need a more sociologically and politically informed perspective on what shapes these emotional lives.

We endorse Hargreaves's position that teaching is an

emotional practice and an intersubjective process involving emotional understanding. Our examples in this chapter powerfully illustrate both this assertion and another assertion we share with Hargreaves: that teachers' emotions are inseparable from their moral purposes.

Sadly, the 'power dynamics of classrooms which separate many teachers' emotional experiences on one side of the desk from students' experiences on the other' (Hargreaves, 1998, p. 839) often lead to an inaccurate emotional understanding and a lack of relationship. Teaching 'other people's children' and failing to engage with difference also impedes emotional understanding.

The perspectives we want to engender

For us, writing this book has been an emotional process in which we have sought to explore, develop and share our interpersonal understandings of rich pedagogy that has communication and relationship at its heart. We do not apologize for our passionate views on the way teaching and learning should be. This is informed by practice, research and reflection and also, of course, at the centre, by what we value in education. In this spirit, we end this chapter with a summary of the perspectives we want to engender.

We want to see an orientation towards learners based on warmth and respect. We want to see perspectives that welcome diversity and that value all learners and their differences. In Ainscow's (1999, p. 6) terms, we reject the 'normative lens' in favour of a 'transformative orientation' in which teachers take advantage of diversity as a stimulus for learning and see learners whose progress causes concern as providing feedback and representing 'hidden voices' that can guide teachers' thinking and practice.

In terms of perspectives on the learning process, we want to see a desire for dialogue and a conceptualization of learners as having valid knowledge and as being competent learners. We desire openness and a willingness to re-invent schools, universities and workplaces as learning organizations with flexible, responsive teachers collaborating with each other – and with learners – to enhance reciprocal, lifelong learning.

From our involvement as teachers concerned with the social and communicative aspects of teaching and learning, we are aware that the key resources for learning are ourselves and our learners, and these resources become most powerful as part of an active and interactive social process.

Chapter 7

Collaborative Learning and Collaborative Teaching

In this chapter we make a case for the importance of collaborative learning and collaborative teaching or, more particularly, collaborative learning for students and for teachers. In many ways the preceding chapters have all been about teachers and students collaborating together, seeing the world from each other's perspective and forming relationships that enhance the learning endeavour. As we will go on to elaborate, we believe that good learning is collaborative both because of the centrality of communication for learning and because thinking is, itself, a social practice. In this chapter, as elsewhere in the book, we argue that for learning to be effective it has to be collaborative, with all participants having a shared understanding of both the material being addressed and the ground rules of communication. In looking at communication between teachers and learners and amongst peers, it becomes increasingly obvious that this distinction is largely academic. In truly collaborative communication the roles of teacher and learner are interchangeable.

As we have said throughout this book, effective interpersonal communication is central to a constructivist view of learning. Consequently, communication is at the centre of our individual and collective research. In an asymmetrical relationship with learners, teachers must take the principal responsibility for shaping interaction. It is often the case that as teachers, bound up inevitably in the normal human condition, we are not aware of how we routinely communicate with learners. Teachers are professional communicators and yet, very often neither our training nor the conditions in which we work are conducive to the most effective forms of communication. We need help to take part in self-directed, professional activities that will increase our effectiveness as communicators. A concern about the detrimental effect of barriers to communication, and therefore collaboration, between teachers and learners is at the heart of Janet Collins's research into the educational, social and emotional needs of quiet learners. The students for whom Melanie Nind's Intensive Inter-action was developed were not developmentally ready for much communication with each other, but the developments in their learning were very much linked with the collaborative learning and teaching of their staff for whom reflective dialogue was a key. Whenever we have sought to discover more about a reported innovative approach or excellent practice, we have found that this reflective dialogue has been at the heart.

This chapter is organized into three sections. We begin by defining what we mean by collaborative learning. In section two we justify the importance of collaboration as related to the social practices of communication and thinking. In a break with tradition, we focus as much on communication between teachers as we do on communication between teachers and learners. Section three discusses the benefits of collaborative learning for teachers and learners. Illustrative examples of good practice as well as strategies for implementing and developing collaborative learning are to be found throughout the chapter.

What is collaborative learning?

When we talk about collaborative learning we distinguish it from learning which may be co-operative in nature. To clarify the distinction we draw on Whipple, who – in correspondence with Gamson (1994) – points out that collaborative learning is always co-operative, but that collaboration goes further in con-fronting issues of power and authority. Collaborating is not just working together towards a common end but also working across differences and boundaries. A simple example illustrates the distinction. A group of learners could co-operate to com-plete a large-scale picture. This would involve everyone working towards a common end, namely the completion of the picture. Each person might be involved in a number of practical tasks, perhaps preparing materials, drawing the basic design, applying paint and so on. However, if they were simply doing as they were asked this would be co-operation. By comparison, if the views of the participants were sought and their ideas allowed to influence the final outcome then the process would become collaborative. Thus a willingness to collaborate incorporates a readiness for peers to grant and accept authority over each other's work, for example, in terms of peer appraisal. Collaborative learning can also challenge the traditional view of teachers' authority and the way in which that authority is exercised. In this way collaborative learning can be about revitalizing democracy. As will be discussed further in this chapter, our interest in collaborative learning reflects our concern about power in relationships.

In collaborative learning the goals are shared and achieved only by working together. We maintain that teachers have no option but to work this way. As teachers we cannot achieve our purposes without engaging learners in the shared project of their development. We become much more than technicians when we co-operate and collaborate in this way and when we also work with colleagues. A national survey of collaborative teacher groups for special educational needs in England (Creese *et al.*, 1998) found teacher groups organized by theme, by task, by function and most of all teachers getting together on an *ad hoc* basis to learn from each other. Whilst teachers work and learn together inside classrooms it is sometimes outside of classrooms that powerful alliances are formed. An example of this is Smith-Livdahl *et al.*'s (1995) 'stories from response-centered classrooms', which arise from teachers' annual 'get togethers' in a log cabin to revitalize their learning about their teaching.

Collaboration between adult writers is also commonplace. One only has to consider the number of co-authored books and articles published each year. Indeed, working together on this book has been an extended exercise in collaborative learning. As we said in the Preface, we came originally from different sectors of education. We each brought our unique histories and different views to the task of creating a shared understanding of the nature of learning. During the production of the various drafts of this manuscript we were involved in creating, negotiating and re-negotiating this shared extended understanding.

Unfortunately, whilst there may be strong evidence of collaboration amongst adult peers, opportunities for younger learners to collaborate in formal educational settings remain relatively rare. There appears to be a difference between rhetoric and reality in collaborative learning, which comes down to issues of ethos. When the rhetoric of collaboration is not realized a lot of group work may go on, but this is likely to be working *in* groups not *as* groups; sitting together but working individually on separate tasks. Despite enthusiasm for collaborative learning most classrooms remain lacking in this, partly because it is treated 'as a toolbox of supplementary methods rather than as a new approach to teaching' (Hansen and Stephens, 2000, p. 40). We may find collaborative activity in classrooms, but no institutional culture of collaboration. It is a 'deliberately collaborative teaching community' (Gamson, 1994) that we need to create to realize the potential of collaborative learning (see Chapter 8 of this book).

> In recent decades, pedagogy has emphasized techniques to the neglect of its moral roots. Under those circumstances, even growth-oriented teaching approaches such as collaborative learning have been treated more as methods than as mind-sets.
>
> (Hansen and Stephens, 2000, p. 47)

In this book our concern with collaborative learning extends beyond our interest in good technique. Like Hansen and Stephens (2000), we view collaborative learning as being at the heart of learner-centred education and central to our purpose in pursuing key humanistic ideals of personal growth and development. Our interest in collaborative learning also reflects our concern with collaboration as a human quality. Johnson and Johnson (1987, p. 15) contend that 'co-operation is as basic to humans as the air we breathe' and we are interested in our basic yearning for community. Many studies demonstrate the power of kinship groups' academic and social support and Horn (1997) shows how students actively seek this.

The prevailing mood of society, despite some distinctive trends to the contrary, has been increasingly individualistic and competitive. Similarly, the prevailing ethos of classrooms has been individualistic. They may be dominated by individual work programmes with the message of 'do your own work and don't interfere with others'. The implementation of curriculum initiatives, such as the National Curriculum, also serve to legitimize individualized, often competitive teaching approaches. Ironically, the assessment of key skills in interactive processes such as Communication and Working with Others is accomplished by individual assessment. In this culture, problems in getting along together are individualized rather than treated as classroom processes. Learners are often encouraged to be teacher-dependent, power differences are strong and collaboration is impeded by an inability to get past them (Gamson, 1994).

Hansen and Stephens (2000) see the reasons for the limited spread of collaborative learning as lying within the culture or ethos and a series of dynamics in which students learn helplessness and expect and are expected to have a passive role. They describe a common and troublesome ethos in which both teacher and student 'have the illusion of success and neither wants to replace the comfort of a dependent relationship with the uncertainties of collaborative interaction' (Hansen and Stephens, 2000, p. 41). They maintain that in this culture students are unwilling to self-appraise critically, that they blame others for their poor performance and that they see themselves as clients with a right to comfort rather than to being challenged. This extends into a transactional relationship in which they have low intrinsic motivation and give up quickly after negative feedback. They fixate on the product rather than on the process of learning. Bates (1998) showed how GNVQ students strongly resist 'empowerment' over their own learning, when this amounts only to 'hunting and gathering information', without any real control over the learning process. These students had no personal training or experience in taking responsibility for their own learning and therefore spent 'independent' time having fun and chatting socially.

As part of an 'us-versus-them' mentality, students may lower their effort to the level of the lowest in the group. They may segregate along dividing lines of race, gender, lifestyles and so on and fear discussion of issues related to these. For staff, fear of litigation and of bad press add to the 'silent conspiracy for "playing it safe"' (Hansen and Stephens, 2000, p. 44). In this culture students are seen as recipients of a service and of knowledge rather than as creators of it. Just as Hansen and Stephens (2000) view these negatives in this light, they view the answers as lying with establishing a collaborative ethos linked to a strong moral purpose.

In contrast to this somewhat bleak picture, collaborative classrooms, have a 'radically different social climate' in which '*everyone* in the classroom is both a teacher and a learner' (Hart, 1996, p. 19: emphasis supplied). Collaboration and community are valued in their own right, problems are shared and structures created that will help to overcome them, and positive action is empowered. Students in collaborative settings are learning the meaning of 'civic responsibility' (Gamson, 1994, p. 49).

We, too, view the collaborative ethos as powerful. We also think of schools and colleges as problem-solving organizations where the notion of work is vaguely defined. We maintain that the work of both teachers and learners is about innovation, experimentation and risk-taking and that an inclusive and collaborative ethos is essential to this. The staff of Cleves School (1999) describe their inclusive school ethos as being about co-operation and collaboration and not competition (p. 53). For them, as for us, learners are helped to share and co-operate through seeing teachers' examples of this in team teaching, which in turn gives teachers the confidence base from which they will welcome and exchange challenging new ideas. The Cleves school culture includes an awareness of the interdependency of the participants of the school community, with everyone understanding that they need to learn to give and accept support, together developing knowledge and understanding of other people, actively learning and making decisions. Their belief that working together collaboratively leads to success and that interdependency creates a sense of belonging and lessens selfishness and insecurity is evident throughout their structures. This is an example of working towards the kind of learning community that we consider in Chapter 8.

Why should learning be collaborative?

Throughout this book we argue that learning should be collaborative because two key aspects of learning, namely communication and thinking, are both social activities carried out between and among people.

The role of conversation in collaborative action research and its value for collaboration and thinking are discussed by Feldman (1999). He reflects on three examples of groups of teachers who get together to converse about their practice as teachers and illuminates some of the beneficial processes at work. The most formal of these is Cochran-Smith and Lytle's (1993) account of teachers building on one another's insights to analyse and interpret data and experiences. These 'oral inquiry processes' are more than just teacher talk in that the communication is self-conscious, self-critical and systematic. They might begin with a 'descriptive review' of a child causing concern and work out to children in general and larger issues.

The second of Feldman's examples is Hollingsworth's (1994) 'collaborative conversations' between urban literacy teachers about 'practice-based concerns'. These conversations helped the teachers to discover their 'biographical connections and differences', to value their lived experiences and to share and generate understandings. Conversation here generated 'relational knowledge', which became 'clarified in action'.

The third example is Feldman's own group of Physics teachers who get together for 'anecdote-telling', 'trying out ideas' and 'systematic inquiry'. Feldman regards the anecdote-telling as the primary mechanism in their 'enhanced normal practice', i.e. practice which is enhanced by a process of sharing stories of practice, listening, questioning and developing relational knowledge. This is the least formal example of communication, which he simply calls 'long and serious conversations', in which knowledge and understanding are generated and shared.

It is the communicative characteristics of conversation that connect the activity of these teachers with the collaborative principle: conversation occurs between and among people, as a co-operative venture, with a direction, but not governed by the clock; it involves exchange of views and connected remarks with contributions 'dovetailed' and 'mutually dependent'. Feldman quotes Searle (1992, pp. 21–2): 'conversations are a paradigm of collective behaviour . . . when two people greet each other and begin a conversation, they are beginning a joint activity rather than two individual activities'. This joint activity involves ideas colliding and mingling and becoming more shared and complex. The direction is not governed by any one participant, but arises via a hermeneutical process. Conversation has a reciprocal quality; it can generate unintended and unpredictable outcomes and can answer questions that have not been asked.

Feldman (1999, p. 133) explores the relationship between conversation and action. Conversation is not a prelude or postscript to action. Conversation can lead to action, follow action or be a part of action. 'It is the recognition of what is alien and opposed to them, and the attempts to recognize the full value of them, that makes conversation critical' (Feldman, 1999, p. 138). We can connect with Feldman's conclusion that in such action research projects, however informal, conversation is a process of inquiry and meaning-making that also helps to develop bonds by providing pleasure. We can relate this to ourselves in our various research projects and in the process of writing this book. What makes us uncomfortable is how little conversation may occur in schools and other learning institutions.

However, as the following example from Janet Collins's research illustrates, even Key Stage Two (7–11-year-olds) learners are capable of insightful and educative conversations. Following a session which drew on a discussion of the film *My Left Foot* by Christy Brown and reference to the work of Stephen Hawking, the class considered the way in which stereotypical ideas about people with disabilities often emphasize the disability and ignore people's strengths and achievements. The class were then introduced to the idea that families often experience difficulties in trying to find mainstream school places for children with disabilities. Citing a particular example of a boy with multiple disabilities, the pupils were asked to consider whether or not such pupils would be better being educated in a mainstream school or a special school. The children were asked to draw on personal experiences and those of friends or family during their discussion.

The pupils were then given fifteen minutes to work with their chosen 'talk partners' and, having arrived at a decision, be prepared to support this with as many reasons as possible. Some groups were asked to tape-record their discussion. At the end of fifteen minutes the class were organized into three feedback groups and their discussion recorded. The success of this activity and the main features of this approach can best be illustrated through an examination of one pupil's contribution to the discussion (Roxana is not her real name).

First, the initial work with talk partners gave Roxana the opportunity to practise telling her story to supportive friends before being faced with the large feedback group. Consequently, without any support beyond the opportunity to practise in advance, in the feedback group Roxana's account was far more structured and coherent. Thus telling her story in advance provided her with the opportunity to clarify for herself what she wanted to say. Second, the earlier discussion with talk partners also provided pupils with something specific to contribute. In this case each pair had written a list of reasons why pupils with disabilities should be educated in mainstream schools. Admittedly the discussion began rather woodenly with pupils taking it in turns to read from their list. In the transcripts that follow Roxana is indicated by the initials RC.

RC   Say one thing and then you pass round.
NM   No. Just say all of them.
SD   'Cos they don't want people to feel sorry for them.
MS   They would like to be with people who have no disability.
NC   They want to be educated like us and be able to get a good job.

As the group continued talking for a total of twenty minutes without intervention from a teacher, it was possible to see how the strategy of taking turns round the circle provided an opportunity for everyone to speak and formed an important starting point for the subsequent discussion. We are convinced that such strategies for initiating discussion should not be underestimated, especially as they can, as on this occasion, provide an opening for pupils to set their own agenda. When the pupils have introduced the topic by reading from their notes they begin to swap anecdotes about disabled people they know. Interestingly, the discussion becomes more animated when Roxana asks a question that introduces a new dimension that seems to have particular importance to her:

> RC   Like say if you were pregnant and you'd just found out that if it were going to be disabled well like would you divorce it . . .
> OC   Abortion.
> RC   . . . have it abortioned like. What would you do Natasha?

It is significant that Roxana is so intent on finding an answer to her question that she hardly notices when one of the other pupils corrects her terminology. As each of the pupils, including Natasha, a confident and accepted leader within the class, gives a negative response to this question, Roxana remains quiet. When it is her turn to speak she passes the debate to the next person in the circle:

> NM   I would have my baby no matter what. You know my baby could come out with two heads like it could even be Siamese twins but I'd still have it.
> RC   What do you think? What would you do?
> MA   I'd have it.

It is only when Owen suggests an alternative answer that Roxana is prepared to suggest her view that an abortion might be an humane way to reduce suffering:

> OC   If it were right brain damaged and it couldn't do anything at all only sit there, and it couldn't see right . . . I'd have it killed [several girls say ah!]
> OC   Life isn't worth living.

RC   No. Same with me right. I would like . . . if it were really
going to be in pain for the rest of its life I wouldn't have it
because it's not really fair on it.
PP   It wouldn't be fair for it, suffering for all of its life.
NC   Yeah, but just think if you have a child . . .
RC   But you wouldn't like your child to be in pain all through
the rest of its life would you?

This illustrates Roxana's self-confidence in forming her own
opinion despite strong peer group pressure, especially from
Natasha, to conform. Moreover, whilst Roxana is not confident
enough openly to contradict her friends, she is quick to develop
Owen's suggestion, which indicates a growing confidence in her
relationships with others. Even when the discussion becomes
heated, Roxana retains her self-confidence and continues to put
forward her own point of view. Whatever we may think about
the content, this episode of pupil talk illustrates many of the
features of successful small group discussions. The tone of the
pupils' contributions and the way in which they support their
views with anecdotes from their own experience suggests that
they have been able to generate a genuine interest in the subject
being discussed. In addition, by asking their own questions they
control and direct the shape of the conversation. They are able
to use their own language and experience in order to name their
world. Moreover, the fact that they can disagree with each other
and correct each other's mistakes without giving or taking
offence suggests that, in this context, they have established a
warm and trusting relationship.

Although we want children to be naturally co-operative,
whatever the task, initially we need to provide tasks that require
co-operation to support their learning of required skills. We also
need to reinforce appropriate competencies in naturalistic situations such as the one above.

The social practice of thinking

We have argued that collaborative learning is effective because
of the importance of communication and interpersonal connec-

tion. We expand this now by emphasizing thinking as a social practice.

Bruner and Haste's transactional model (Cooper and McIntyre, 1994, p. 637) explains the sharing and testing of intersubjective meanings, the negotiation of interpretations through interaction and the exercise of sympathy that is enabled through the provision of 'grammars and scripts' and 'scaffolding'. In this model, cognitive development is highly dependent on sociocultural influences, on certain types of interpersonal and social interaction and on congenial circumstances. Processes at work include the 'calibration' mechanism – the careful matching of intersubjectivities, testing understandings held by one another, adjusting to make them accessible to each other and mutual assistance to achieve overlapping zones of proximal development. This is a continual and recursive process.

A powerful example of thinking as a social practice comes from Naysmith and Palma's (1998) discussion of the problems teachers involved with their action research had with writing as a means for reflection, compared with the ease and enjoyment of their talk and interaction. The participants regarded the group as the engine powering their ability to reflect. The teachers viewed themselves as 'fundamentally practitioners', as 'practical people' (Manuela in group, p. 68), doing their reflections holistically whilst on the job. With the group's talk, however, they valued 'the possibility of sharing experiences' (Manuela, p. 71), the potential for mutual support, the potential for sympathizing and empathizing and the way in which ideas could be produced jointly. They valued the social contact, the immediate feedback, the way the group allowed humour and 'a "social" approach to a "serious" task' (p. 73).

Co-operative talk enables the testing out of ideas, the use of tentative expression and the expression of contradictions that would require more careful wording when written and stored. Naysmith and Palma (1998, p. 73) postulate: 'talk is a social activity, writing is not; thought is "scaffolded" by spoken interaction'. They conclude that 'the group itself and the oral interaction between participants appears to have enabled reflection on action to have become a dynamic social activity which has led to the collaborative construction of meaning' (p. 73). This social co-construction of knowledge is at the heart of collaborative learning and teaching and Naysmith and Palma's insights are valuable ones. Whilst we would disagree that writing is not social – writing this book together has been an example of writing as a social activity in which knowledge is co-constructed – we acknowledge that we have valued our face-to-face talk most highly in the process.

What are the benefits of collaborative learning?

Gamson (1994, p. 45) summarizes the positive outcomes of collaborative learning as follows: 'complexity of thinking increases, as does acceptance of different ideas; motivation for learning goes up; a sense of connection among students, even when they are quite different from one another, is enhanced'. Collaboration reduces isolation and leads to more student-centred classrooms, with companionship, support, greater sources of feedback, new ideas, greater energy, more active participation. There is also evidence that collaborative learning improves student retention (Gamson, 1994), which is all the more significant when we recall the bleak statistics for truanting and dropout cited in Chapter 1.

In Chapter 4, we asserted how important peer interaction may be in boosting motivation to learn and modelling effective learning (Azmitia, 1998). Fundamentally, human beings are collaborative creatures. We have survived, often in adversity, by working together, and our use of language, as Habermas (1986) has pointed out, posits a fundamental bond between persons that enables us to reach consensus. Many of the features of collaborative learning echo the dimensions of good learning we stress in Chapter 1 and throughout this book: these are active and interactive participation, intrinsic motivation, rich communication, trusting relationship and the potential to transform thinking and lives.

Collaborative learning is productive

All of Brufee's (1994) motivations for current interest in collaborative learning connect with our motivations. Evidence that students learn better when they learn collaboratively is important to us. The rationale that the rest of the world is now working collaboratively relates to the connection we are making between good pedagogy and lifelong learning. The understanding that knowledge is socially constructed and learning occurs among persons rather than between a person and things is central to our model of learning. The need for teamwork in adulthood is hard to dispute and the logic of teaching teamwork and effective interdependence at school is well recognized. This chapter is about how learning is not an individual process but a social one. We show how collaborative learning combined with collaborative pedagogy provides powerful challenges to assumptions about how knowledge is created and leads to deeper appreciation of this social construction of meaning.

In all kinds of teaching and learning we can achieve so much more together than we ever could alone. Both student–student support and teacher–teacher support are under-used resources and should be mobilized. In drives toward inclusive education this realization has been key. Proponents of inclusive education have had to consider how we can do more in education for more people. Ainscow (1999) and Mittler (2000) amongst others have argued that we can learn much from poorer countries where peer support is readily used. Ainscow (1995, p. 149) maintains that 'within any classroom the pupils represent a rich source of experiences, inspiration, challenge and support which, if utilized, can inject an enormous supply of additional energy'. Johnson and Johnson (1987, p. 2) have noted how influential student–student interaction is on performance, peer interactions being more frequent, intense and varied than teacher–student interaction. In this book, of course, we are concerned with enriching all teaching and learning interactions, and this involves us with the dynamics of power.

The situations that Hansen and Stephens (2000) argue are responsible for the interest in collaborative learning in higher education we find to be true in a broader sense. Research on learning and teaching effectiveness confirms the efficacy of learner-driven approaches in schools as well as higher education (HE) institutions. Moves towards inclusive schooling make school as well as HE student populations increasingly diverse and this diversity calls for creative responses to foster student engagement. The demands of the rapidly changing information society mean that flexible and team-based competencies need to be addressed in schools well in advance of the HE phase. Lastly, whilst we may debate whether a political climate in which teaching philosophies 'empower' students and make classrooms more democratic really exists currently in schools, we contend that this should be so.

Collaborative learning is non-competitive

There is ample research evidence showing that students learn better through non-competitive group work than in classrooms that are highly individualized and competitive (Johnson and Johnson, 1987; Brufee, 1994). The research of Tinto and Good-sell-Love (1993), for example, filled a gap in terms of empirical evidence for the claims of enhanced participation and achievement when collaborative learning is facilitated in HE. Their study of two very different American HE institutions with distinctive collaborative programmes showed that students in the collaborative learning programmes were more involved, had more positive attitudes, viewed the quality of learning differently, persisted more and had higher performance than the non-participants. This was true even in the traditional institution with a small venture into facilitating peer collaboration. In the institution with non-traditional HE students, where the programme involved both collaborative learning and collaborative teaching and made positive use of a diversity of students and student experience, there were also high levels of active learning and reflection on learning.

Cognitive, social and affective benefits of collaborative learning are all reported and Johnson and Johnson (1987) conclude:

> There is a great deal of research to indicate that if student–
> student interdependence is structured carefully and appropriately,

students will achieve at a higher level, more frequently use higher level reasoning strategies, have higher levels of academic motivation, be more intrinsically motivated, develop more positive interpersonal relationships with each other, value more the subject area being studied, have higher self-esteem, and be skilled interpersonally.

(Johnson and Johnson, 1987, p. 9)

They emphasize positive interdependence in co-operative learning, which is linked with acceptance, support, trust and liking of peers, exchange of information, oral rehearsal of ideas, mutual influence, high use of resources, intrinsic motivation, high commitment and high emotional involvement in learning (Johnson and Johnson, 1987, p. 29). Hart (1996) adds to the social and cognitive benefits, benefits in management and pedagogy because enabling students to be less dependent on teachers creates opportunities for more quality, sustained teacher–student interaction.

By comparison, individualized and competitive situations, such as those engendered by the introduction of National Curriculum Assessments, can place children under enormous pressure and can have a negative effect on children's perceptions of themselves and their peers (Reay and Wiliam, 1999).

We actually know more about the benefits of collaborative learning than we understand about how and why those benefits occur. Brufee (1994, p. 45) proposes that collaborative learning 'calls on levels of ingenuity and inventiveness that many students never knew they had'. Gamson (1994) suggests we can understand the process using group process theories and theories about 'connected learning', 'situated cognition' and social constructivism. Greenhalgh (1994) begins to unpick how the development of higher quality cognitive strategies through co-operative learning methods happens. He notes 'the improvement of understanding through discussion and controversy; the improvement of long-term retention through continual restatement and reformulation of new ideas; the enrichment of ideas through exchanges between pupils of different background, achievement levels and experiences; and the increase in motivation for learning' (Greenhalgh, 1994, p. 196).

Collaborative learning affects relationships

What becomes clear from this discussion is that communication and relationship are mutually dependent and integral to learning. This is further illustrated by Horn's (1997) study of American college students supporting each other personally and academically in learning communities. Horn (1997, p. 27) discusses the academic and social skills learned in collaboration, including 'goal-setting, negotiation of authority, personal responsibility, persistence, inductive and deductive approaches to learning, creative and logical application of new information, interdependence with students of different backgrounds'. She maintains that these are abilities 'that should put them in a position to succeed, not only in their current courses but also in their future careers' (p. 27). Central to her argument, and ours, is that whilst the most effective students may intuit the worth of collaborations and use them extensively, we should actively teach at-risk students to do the same, thus breaking the isolation and creating peer groups that are immersed in the learning process.

At its best student–student support is mutual and so has advantages over one-way traditional teacher-to-student, advisor-to-student or expert-to-novice support. We need to foster supportive kinships that spend time in constructive, collaborative activities, learning how to study and how to manage their complicated lives as students with other roles. We need to teach and model collaborative learning and provide the supportive atmosphere in which it can flourish.

We also need to develop situations in which teachers and pupils can collaborate together in their own learning. Situations in which the teacher has to admit that he or she is still learning and does not know all the answers can be threatening. This is an issue that goes beyond important and sensitive issues of classroom discipline. When pupils are encouraged to ask questions, invariably they will raise subjects beyond the expertise of the teacher. Teachers are no longer able to maintain an image of themselves as the custodians of all knowledge. Whilst this image is, by definition, both unrealistic and false, it protects

individuals from addressing what they fear are their own inadequacies as a teacher.

The way in which teachers can be threatened by pupils'
insatiable curiosity is illustrated in a poignant fictional episode in
Petals of Blood, by Ngugi wa Thiong'o (1977). Godfrey Munira
teaches in the village school. One day he takes his pupils out
into the open air for a botany lesson in which he aims to provide
the pupils with 'hands on' experiential learning. He teaches the
children the names of the flowers and the names of their
constituent parts and he feels proud to be imparting hard,
factual, reliable information. But the fragile social order between
himself and the children is maintained by nothing more substantial than his factual knowledge and his academic language. It
begins to crumble when the children use vivid poetic metaphors
to describe the flowers, when they notice that some flowers are
worm-eaten and when they ask disquieting questions about why
beauty gets destroyed and why God allows it to happen. His
answer that it is all the laws of nature does not satisfy the
children and they respond with formidable questions about
humankind, law, God and nature:

> Man . . . law . . . God . . . nature: he had never thought deeply
> about these things, and he swore that he would never again take
> the children to the fields. Enclosed in the four walls he was the
> master, aloof, dispensing knowledge to a concentration of faces
> looking up to him. There he could avoid being drawn in . . . But
> out in the fields, outside the walls, he felt insecure.
>
> (Thiong'o, 1977, p. 22)

Like Munira, we need to learn how to handle passionate
reflection, dialogue and argument amongst our learners, for
learning cannot be confined to classrooms, didactic instruction
and deferential note-taking. We also need to risk ourselves in the
collaborative pursuit of understanding.

Collaborative learning changes power relationships

As the above example illustrates, collaborative learning can
change the power relationships between teachers and learners. It

also has an impact on relationships among peers. Ewing and Kennedy (1996) found the following gains associated with co-operative learning: children recognizing the importance of relationships with each other, appreciating each other's view-point, recognizing the need for combined effort, being aware of each individual's unique contribution, being concerned for others and being able to act as leaders, organizers and mediators. They identify the features of co-operative learning as being central to the process in which such benefits are accrued. The process of peers working together to achieve shared goals, where there is individual accountability, corporate responsibility, shared leadership and positive interdependence, requires skilled and appropriate use of interpersonal skills. This necessitates the teaching, learning or practising of a range of abilities in communication, the building and maintenance of trust, peer tutoring, leadership and handling of controversy.

These interpersonal relationships in classrooms are fascinating to us. Moreover, we endorse Gamson's (1994) important observation that collaborative classrooms transform the students and teachers within them. They are changed such that they cannot then go back and be the people they were before they were touched by the rich social and interactive process of being teachers and learners together. Exploring how and why this happens enhances our value as teachers.

The power of the collaborative ethos

We can begin to understand the importance of an ethos of collaborative learning when we look at its role in emotional development. One of our central tenets of learning is that we need to be able to practise in safety with appropriate levels of security and challenge. Greenhalgh (1994) explains how in a group we can receive feedback about our own participation and behaviour, which facilitates our personal growth. We can observe what happens to others when they make challenges and we can try out new behaviours in an exploratory way. Groups with interdependence allow learners to feel valued, for themselves and for their contribution, and to experience shared influence.

In showing how collaborative group work can be a powerful tool for enabling positive interaction and personal development, Greenhalgh (1994) uses a 'churning' analogy, with images of turning over ideas in the mind and of rubbing up against each other in continuous action long enough to bring about change. If individuals do not feel safe in the group, they will flee or psychologically insulate themselves, by, for example, interacting only with the leader or with subgroups or doing solitary activities. These strategies, though, mean avoiding the risk of emotional growth. The therapeutic process, he explains, is enhanced when every group member is a giver and not just a receiver of help, and by an ethos in which group members can work through process issues of safety (Will I be emotionally and physically safe in the group?), acceptance (Will I be liked or disliked? How will I be treated?) and participation (What will my place in the group be?).

As Hansen and Stephens (2000) stress, learning and teaching demand courage; students and teachers need to take risks when entering unknown territory. For the trust needed for this to happen they need a sense of caring, a sense of justice and a sense of accountability as a moral obligation. A collaborative ethos means that collaborative learning and teaching can be more than isolated techniques. Collaboration can enable emotional and personal involvement – making active connections with others – and therefore engender emotional and personal growth. Similarly, active engagement with learning material helps to ensure that learning is intrinsically motivating. Personal involvement and active engagement are also central to enabling the rich communication that is essential to learning.

Chapter 8

Collaborating in Learning Communities

In the previous chapter we discussed the importance of collaboration between teachers and learners to enhance the quality of learning. In this chapter we develop (1) the principle that good learning is active and interactive and (2) outline the context required for this to happen, by venturing into the terrain of learning communities. Our premise that learning is social and that communication and relationship are at the heart of good learning fits well with emerging concepts of learning communities. Before we consider current thinking in this arena, however, we must remember that learning communities, both inside and outside the classroom, have long been an issue for educators. Schools have long been seen as places where young learners are introduced to the beliefs, ideals and habits of communities of readers, linguists, scientists, mathematicians, etc., in the wider society. However, Dewey's comment on education in the 1890s still holds true in our current educational institutions:

> I believe that much of present education fails because it neglects this fundamental principle of the school as a form of community life. It conceives the school as a place where certain information is to be given, where certain lessons are to be learned, or where certain habits are to be formed. The value of these is conceived as lying largely in the remote future; the child must do these things for the sake of something else he is to do; they are mere preparation. As a result they do not become part of the life experience of the child and so are not truly educative.
>
> (Dewey, 1897, p. 8)

The concept of a learning community

If we are saying that learners and teachers need to communicate with each other, relate to each other and work together towards common goals, then are we saying that we need to form learning communities of some kind and if we are what do we mean by this? As a current buzzword, claims to being a learning community abound but in the literature the concept of a 'learning community' is at present relatively unformed, as is that of a 'community of practice' (Wenger, 1998).

Sergiovanni (1999, p. 16) draws on the distinction of Tonnies between *Gemeinschaft* and *Gesellschaft*, i.e. community as distinct from society. Community (*Gemeinschaft*) has characteristics such as people sharing emotional ties, values and beliefs through frequent interaction, leading to a commitment to a particular place and history. Productive learning communities, according to Sergiovanni, are characterized by features in which both students and teachers are:

- *reflective* about how they learn;
- *developmental* in developing at different rates with varying readiness for particular learning;
- *diverse* with different talents catered for;
- *conversational* with exchanges of values and ideas;
- *caring* through helping one another to grow as learners and as persons; and
- *responsible* with all participants seeing themselves as socially responsible actors.

For Sergiovanni, the creation of a learning community requires students and teachers to work together in teams, in the pursuit of shared goals, over an extended period of time. In this account, the concept of leadership is rooted in professional and moral authority, established by open agreement on values and norms in a climate that is harmonious. In contrast, leadership that is rooted in bureaucracy or personal authority and in which the goals of the leader are not synonymous with those of the led will not result in learning communities.

A variation of this concept is proposed by Retallick (1999), who holds that the concept of a 'learning community' is a metaphor 'that helps us organize and pursue a new vision of education' (Retallick, 1999, p. 110). Starratt (1996) identifies three main characteristics of a learning community. First, that learning is situated in a critical community of inquirers who share understandings. Second, that the learning agenda necessarily explores questions important to individuals and to the social life and cultural projects of the time. Finally, that the learning is continuously related to students' everyday lives. These relate closely to our emphasis on learners' perspectives and on teaching and learning as a coalition between all participants.

Learning communities then may take many different forms and display divergent characteristics; however, Starratt's (1996) 'beginning listing' of the processes of forming learning communities summarized below is useful. In a learning community, learning should

- take place in a caring environment, marked by the relationships between participants and by the co-operative processes of learning;
- involve a lot of storytelling to link formal learning and personal life;
- relate to home and neighbourhood experiences;
- lead to some product or performance to show the usefulness of learning to the school and the wider community;
- refer to the 'meta-narratives' of our culture that give coherent meaning to new knowledge; and
- explore the biggest questions about what it is to be human and to be a community.

We have considered these characteristics and processes in classrooms in formal learning, but in learning communities they should be practised across whole educational institutions, rather than occurring in pockets. Grubb (1999) found that more innovative practices in US Community Colleges often existed without the knowledge of institution management and without effect on the practices of institutions as a whole. The challenge of learning communities is to institutionalize learning, i.e. to define and build the community capabilities and structures (such as culture, processes, systems and skills) necessary for learning (Hutchens, 1998). As teachers we may be happy to stop at fostering collaboration in our classrooms, or we may want to foster collaboration and learning community for our institutions, thus maximizing individual and group energy through collective effort.

For us, a preoccupation with the quality of learning leads us to aspire to encourage learning communities. Senge *et al.* (1994) refer to learning communities as 'deep learning cycles' in which the members and the community itself are changed by it. Learning communities are centres for transformational learning. In the milieu of trusting relationships and synergy, members of learning communities develop in terms of awareness and sensibilities, skills and capabilities and attitudes and beliefs.

Fostering learning communities

The creation of learning communities is considered by Wenger (1998, p. 237) who holds that this depends on a dynamic combination of three factors:

- engagement – opportunities to contribute actively to the practices of communities that we value and that value us;
- imagination – processes of orientation, reflection and exploration to place our identities and practices in a broader context; and
- alignment – frameworks of convergence, co-ordination and conflict resolution that determine the social effectiveness of our actions.

This social view of learning, derived from Wenger's observations of how people learn in non-formal settings, gives rise to a vision of education that is at variance with most current practice. Learning in naturalistic settings inevitably involves building complex social relationships around meaningful activities. Spontaneous development of a learning community would involve a genuine taking charge of learning as the enterprise of that community. Deliberate fostering of a learning community involves an infrastructure incorporating activities that require mutual engagement, both among students and with other people involved, just as fostering of collaborate learning involves activities that require joint effort. There would need to be challenges and responsibilities that draw on students' existing knowledge and encourage them to explore new territories. There would also need to be 'enough continuity for participants to develop shared practices and a long-term commitment to their enterprise and to each other' (Wenger, p. 272).

For Wenger, as for us, the fact that we are social beings is of central importance for how we learn. This has implications in that knowledge becomes about competence in doing things that we value, which requires 'active engagement in the world' and 'our ability to experience the world and our engagement with it as meaningful' (Wenger, p. 4). Learning is inherent in human nature, is fundamentally experiential and social and is first and foremost the ability to negotiate new meanings. Individuals embody community in their nature; the sense of self is found in relationships with others where individuals become more fully human. The learning community forms a living system, a pattern of interactions in which, facilitated by language, we interpret our experiences in a myriad of ways.

Learning communities require enough structure and continuity to accumulate experience and enough perturbation and discontinuity to continually renegotiate meaning. They transform our identities by building personal histories in relation to the histories of our communities and creating bridges and boundaries between our multi-membership of various communities (e.g. school, home, work).

Learning is a matter of social energy and power and so

it is more important for students to have experiences that allow them to take charge of their own learning than to cover a lot of material. A curriculum would then look more like an itinerary of transformative experiences of participation than a list of subject

> matter. Given enough resources, the practice of a learning
> community can become rich and complex enough to be the
> driving force of a complete education.
>
> (Wenger, 1998, p. 272)

When we compare this with the learning in formal education, where experiences are so often disengaged from the practical competences of our experiences outside schooling, it is no wonder that so many young people are disengaged from school, either physically through absence or meta-physically by their thoughts and longings being elsewhere. Education should provide structure for learning or what Wenger refers to as 'reification' – the mission statements of values and norms, the protocols for getting things down; and at the same time genuine opportunities for 'participation' – acting, interacting, mutuality. Structures with too little participation are bureaucratic shells; participation without structure may be experienced as chaos. Both structure and participation are needed in balance.

So far as contemporary education is concerned we do not believe we have the balance right. As the Fryer Report (1997) on Lifelong Learning recognized, we have created structures – of curriculum, assessment and inspection – that place far too much emphasis on bureaucracy (often ramshackle and underfunded) and in consequence far too little on participation. Hence, it is common for people to refer to education in contradistinction to the 'real world', which, by definition lies outside. Why should learners be expected to leave the real world and endure a structure that fails so many and palpably does not meet the human needs of so many more? How can a formal education that is 'outside life' promote 'lifelong learning'?

Power and participation

The problem of education does not lie with teachers. We are often constrained, often against our better judgement, to work within structures that we believe to be antithetical to learning. The problem lies at a much deeper level and may be compared with granting the franchise. In the nineteenth century in England it was considered unthinkable by many to give the vote to non-property-owning men. In the early twentieth century it was considered unthinkable (by many men who would not have been granted a vote a century earlier) that women should be given the franchise. In the twenty-first century in England many people would regard it as the end of civilization to grant real power over their lives to young people in education. They are not mature enough to act responsibly; they have too little experience of the world; they would want things that are not good for them. Basically, other (older, wiser, more experienced) people know best. This fear of young people may be understandable – it is in essence the same fear as aristocrats had for the masses or colonials for subject people – there are many of them (students) and few of us (teachers). What if they get out of control? A desire or need to be, and to be seen to be, in control lies at the heart of all oppressive practices. It may be predicted, however, that just as it now appears absurd that most people, including all women, were once not able to vote, it will one day appear absurd that children and young people had little or no voice in their own education.

Learner empowerment and autonomy; the learning society; the learning age; learning organizations; lifelong learning – are all familiar contemporary buzzwords. We argue, however, that they lack meaning without the kind of genuine participation outlined in this book. So, what do genuine participation and learning community look, and feel like, in practice?

Sharnbrook Upper School in Bedfordshire has worked hard for many years to engage learners in activities and conversations that give them real power over processes of teaching and learning. Staff of the school are aware that involving students in, for example, councils and feedback about teaching can be tokenistic. Determined to move beyond this to genuine empowerment, the school has a democratically elected Council, with representation from all years, and a policy of embracing the views of all parts of the school community, including students who do not seem to want to take part because 'no one ever listens to them'. A senior student chairs the Council; staff attend by invitation; and the Council sends representatives to the

Organizing Bureau of European School Student Unions (OBESSU).

Students at Sharnbrook are involved in all staff appointments and in the formulation of all school policies. Many students are part of a 'students as researchers' programme (cf. the terminology of www.notschool.net below), which, among other things, has researched teaching and learning issues and given rise to a process of giving supportive feedback about teaching to trainees in initial teacher training and to newly qualified teachers. It is hoped that this scheme will be extended to all teaching staff.

OBESSU, which is not widely represented in British schools, is a long-standing organization that is funded by the European Union. OBESSU has a European School Student Rights Charter that may one day seem as unthreatening as the demands of the Tolpuddle martyrs. Here we give a flavour of the Charter by quoting one example from each article:

1.2 In every school there should be a legally recognized student council, which has been democratically elected by the school students.

2.5 School students must have at least equal influence as teachers have in the school decision-making processes.

3.1 School students should have the right to appeal against unfair treatment and have the right to demand disciplinary actions in case of such violations.

4.2 Education must be based upon mutual respect, understanding, democracy and tolerance. School systems will promote the fight against discrimination, fascism and xenophobia.

5.6 Every type of education at secondary level should contain general education.

6.3 School students should not be required to specialize before they are fully aware of the importance and impact of their choice.

7.2 The individuality of school students must be respected by the school. Equality in education shall not mean uniformity: students have to be allowed to develop their personal abilities towards the direction they want to.

8.1 Discrepancy in skills between school students because of a gender-specific socialization should be compensated by means of education. Schools will actively work for gender equality in society.

9.2 Education and learning should not be regarded as occurring only during the years in school. The school system should adapt itself to serve the principle of continuous education. Students must be taught abilities and given facilities to actively seek information themselves and not only to receive knowledge passively through the teaching process.

10.2 The social function of the school should be taken into account and cared for.

11.3 School students should be informed about everything that is of relevance for their education and its procedures. Plans for each subject in the curriculum should be presented to the school students before the beginning of each term.

12.1 In every school there shall be a set of internal regulations. The school board or the school community will decide upon the content of these rules. In unclear cases, the interpretation of the regulations shall be done by the school board, not by the headmaster or teachers.

13.1 School students have the right to receive education in areas that are of importance for understanding the world we live in, such as:

- intercultural education
- sex education
- education promoting democratic participation in society
- environmental education
- tolerance and solidarity
- social skills.

14.1 To safeguard that – once adopted – the contents of this charter are properly used and that the legislation concerning the school student rights is being followed, it is of the greatest importance that there are supervising authorities at every level that are competent to take disciplinary actions against the party which is in violation.

Notable in this Charter, in keeping with other demands for rights over the past centuries, is that the school students are not mildly requesting that schools and teachers grant them things, if it is acceptable to those in authority. Young people who believe that they should have a real voice in their own education – its nature, quality and assessment – are demanding power here. They demand a genuine partnership with teachers and not a token presence on the school governing body.

If there is to be genuine community, then, as we have seen, there must be active participation by all. Only by creating structures that permit student voice about learning, as a routine part of educational life, can there be such a thing as a learning community. Some countries are experimenting with ways in which to re-make education along more democratic lines. Fogelman (1997) cites as an example a booklet issued to Norwegian secondary students, setting out how they should take responsibility for their own learning and participate in student councils. In Sweden, a Youth Act was passed in 1999, requiring all secondary schools to engage learners actively in decisions about education.

It is not only able secondary school students and students in further and higher education who are able to take part in a community of learning. We showed in Chapter 2 how infants are able to negotiate and take much of the lead in the content, tempo and style of their early interactions. We know that very young children are often sophisticated users of language and are able to equivocate, show sensitivity and hold accurate and nuanced views about their education. Some infant schools are experimenting with ways to engage pupils more actively in the process of their own education. For example, Moorings Way Infants School, Portsmouth, helps children to understand their own preferred learning styles:

Boy (age 5)   I'm an intrapersonal learner.
(Head)   What happens when you're an interpersonal learner?
Boy   I get silly.

The Head's philosophy is that teaching is sharing what you know and that there should be openness of communication, in which opinions are valued and applauded whenever possible. 'Specials' are run on topics such as sex education, anger and the budget, as a forum for pupils to express their own views. The guiding principle of these popular meetings is 'at the end of the day it's what they (pupils) say'.

Moll and Whitmore (1998) cite an attempt to apply Vygotskian methods to emphasize active child development. 'In our case study the children select topics for study . . . choose books to read and issues to analyse, specify research questions to address . . . create texts for authentic purposes, and publicly display their learning' (Moll and Whitmore, 1998, p. 152). In this process, control of learning is shared between teacher and students, there is a building of mutual trust and the authenticity of materials and tasks is stressed.

It may be the case that in Britain major private schools provide an example of creating and sustaining learning communities. Oakeshott (1959), who advocated that education be a conversation that is tolerant of different voices, quoted the headmaster (William Cory) of a major English private school, Eton College: 'you go to a great school not so much for knowledge as for arts and habits . . . entering quickly into another person's thoughts . . . submitting to censure and refutation . . . indicating assent or dissent in graduated terms' (Oakeshott, pp. 12–13). By contrast, Rodenburg (1992) recounted working at Eton College where she was 'stunned by the open vocal release and freedom', compared with working in a state comprehensive in a depressed area of London where discussion was minimal; 'it was just slightly short of vocal repression' (p. 8). Again we are reminded of bigger issues of power and control and the need for education to be transformative for all learners.

State control of public education may take a very conservative view of the possibilities for change. Lawley (1999, p. 13), writing of *Education 2000* (a campaign to reform education by better understanding of how people learn in formal and informal settings, and making better links between them), reported that

In a meeting at Downing Street a spokesman for the British
Prime Minister [John Major, Conservative] stated in 1996, 'Your
[Education 2000] ideas are interesting but they require very good
teachers. We are not convinced that there are enough of these so
we have emphasized a "teacher proof" curriculum.' Teaching and

Schools, not Learning and Community, were to become that Government's organizing principles. At the time of writing, and with a Labour government in power, there is no sign that this fundamental conservatism has changed.

Learners who have traditionally lacked power have suffered from the learned helplessness we have discussed in earlier chapters. For people with learning difficulties, however, the self-advocacy movement has helped to reverse this, by providing a forum, a kind of learning community, in which people with learning disabilities have supported each other in the difficult process of finding a voice. Inclusive projects, such as Atkinson's *Life History* project and inclusive research in which women with learning difficulties tell their stories, have enabled some people from a devalued group to *cross a boundary* that has been, and continues to be, drawn between people with learning difficulties and the 'rest of the population' (Jackson, 2000). Adult education projects, such as those described by Stuart and Thomson (1995) and Preece (2000), have similarly made important contributions to enabling the 'other' in education to become lifelong learners in forms of learning communities.

Democracy and autonomy

The challenge of any democracy – large or small – is to give voice to people. Communities, by definition, as distinct from societies, are about shared understandings, based on interpersonal interaction. To create and sustain learning communities, schools, colleges and universities need to find ways to empower people – students and teachers too. Exercising personal powers is central to 'being a person' and to being able to participate in a social world; personal powers are gained in 'negotiated interaction with those who already have them' (Shotter, 1973, p. 154). Participants in learning communities need to be able to be autonomous in order to become interdependent.

We turn briefly here to autonomy and to the taking of personal power. Heathcote (1997) holds that autonomy is based on four values. These are the ability:

- to be self-determining and to 'execute one's own plans';
- to be self-governing, i.e. to be able to 'stand back from one's
  . . . self-interest . . . to take account of others' needs';
- to exercise responsibility for 'one's thoughts and actions,
  particularly as they relate to others'; and
- 'the ability to undertake self-development, and to achieve self-
  realization in ways which engender a sense of coherence in
  one's life, and feelings of self-esteem'.

(Heathcote, 1997, p. 167)

There are echoes here of values we have considered elsewhere in the book.

Just as learning is inevitably social, autonomy is social as well as individual. Heathcote (1997) is clear on this; she draws on Mead's concept of 'I' and 'Me', where the pre-social 'I' is distinguished from the 'Me' in which self-consciousness is developed reflexively in interaction with others. As Kant (1949) maintained, autonomy is not 'so much a quality or characteristic which human beings possess' as an ideal or obligation. 'Respect the autonomous nature of human beings whether in your own person or in that of another.'

These values are negated or made difficult to practise by many forms of oppression: economic, political, social, ideological. To become autonomous in the sense outlined here one must be empowered and this in turn means that someone more powerful must become less powerful. Fielding (1997) points out that the term 'empowerment' is often used without this meaning – thus teachers may be exhorted to become more professional (implying autonomy and empowerment) while at the same time being increasingly constrained by government regulations. There may be rhetoric about empowering learners whilst there is no intention for teachers to give up any of their power. When Coupe-O'Kane *et al.* (1994) discuss individuals with severe learning difficulties learning to take control in their lives, they note that 'it can quickly be seen that elements of tension exist when we consider our own role and how our *own* behaviour might need to change if we aim for our pupils to develop autonomy' (p. 15). Similarly, in order for less vocal learners to be empowered to have a voice in the classroom, there has to be a significant change in the behaviour of teachers and other learners. Encouraging quieter individuals to speak involves everyone recognizing that they not only have the right to speak but also something of value to contribute to the discussion. Moreover, there is a need for those who habitually speak to remain silent and listen (Collins, 1996). Relationships in the classroom have to change.

Human communication is partly based upon who controls interaction (see Chapter 9) and for teachers to empower learners they must yield some of their own power (Coupe-O'Kane *et al.*, 1994). This is difficult to do – it seems risky. Both local and national policy may stress being in control at all times. Empowerment is not even about the more powerful yielding some of their power to the less powerful, for power that is given may be taken away (Williams and Nind, 1999). As Fielding (1997) argues, it is more fundamentally about 'rupturing' present relationships and shaping them anew. It is about 'critical democracy' and, as such, leads us back to Habermas and back too to wider political and philosophical ideas and debates. Power is not a thing or a quantum to be measured; it is a relationship, and some relationships are more positive than others for the humanity of those involved.

One way in which power relationships are being ruptured and reshaped is by teaching and learning through the new technologies using electronic communication and conferencing. A prime example of exploration of this is in the 'notschool' media-rich online learning community. The community is for people who may be disaffected, disruptive, ill or phobic and deliberately avoids the vocabulary of school (pupil, teacher, lesson). There are 'researchers', who are the learners themselves exploring and informing their own development, and there are learning experts who provide researchers with the subject help and learning support they need. The nature of the interactions is allowed to be different; it is acceptable for individuals to join the community at their own pace, to choose not to publicize their level of activity until they are confident, to 'lurk' until ready to contribute. At the same time there is a supportive online community of mentors to ease this process. The interactions also avoid giving and receiving of knowledge, as 'notschool is absolutely not a compendium of content ... community rather than content is king and high quality content springs from the whole community as a result of their engagement' (www.notschool.net).

As this example shows, re-making the nature of relationships in education, in order genuinely to empower learners, goes far beyond 'citizenship' education, although this term may refer to a wide variety of educational practice, from minimal knowledge about rights and politics to more proactive approaches that stress inclusion and build skills to effect change (Fogelman, 1997). The practice of education *as* critical democracy cannot be confined to one curriculum 'subject' entitled Citizenship. Darling-Hammond (1996) remarked how education in the USA is not democratic but actually operates in a way that undermines the ability of individuals to participate actively in a democracy. The Kingman Report into the teaching of English (1988) held that there can be democracy only if people have the ability to use language – which means both the capability of using it and the right to use it:

> People need expertise in language to be able to participate effectively in a democracy ... A democratic society needs people who have the linguistic abilities which will enable them to discuss, evaluate and make sense of what they are told, as well as to take effective action on the basis of their understanding ... Otherwise there can be no genuine participation, but only the imposition of the ideas of those who are linguistically capable.
>
> (Kingman Report, 1988, p.7)

Goduka (1998) makes explicit the vital link between getting heard and getting engaged as learners: 'The process of awakening one's identity and voice is essential for the development of skills for critical engagement and participation' (Goduka, 1998, cited by Preece, 2000, p. 6).

Finding a voice is part of learning how to learn. It is part of discovering what it is to be an active participant in an ongoing learning process. It can lead to reflection on that learning process and more self-aware learning. By engaging with learners' per-spectives we help them to engage critically with their own perspectives – in bell hooks's words (p. 186), 'coming to voice'. As we have pointed out earlier, this may be significantly easier for some learners than for others (Collins, 1996).

The concept of 'critical democracy' cannot be confined to the role of learners. Teachers too need to be empowered or to empower themselves. Johnson (1999) holds that 'a learning community is . . . a community whose culture is characterized by commitment and professionalism. It is a community where the staff's voices are heard, their ideas are valued and they are viewed as professionals' (p. 40). Becoming a learning community requires teachers to work together in teams, perhaps in an 'action learning' model where small groups of colleagues meet regularly to improve their practices (Hoban, 1999, p. 175). One of Senge's (1990) basic learning disciplines, which together are seen to provide vital dimensions in building organizations that can truly 'learn', is team learning, which starts with dialogue and involves suspending assumptions and entering into genuine 'thinking together' (p. 10).

Learning communities online

Virtual classrooms and electronic learning environments are frequently seen as the answers to the challenge of both learning communities and lifelong learning. The information age is both a threat and an opportunity here. There is real danger, given the quantity and availability of information on offer on the worldwide web, of people becoming passive recipients and con-sumers of knowledge as in Freire's (1972) banking model. But there is also a real opportunity to re-think and build alternative communities of learners as in notschool. The Education with New Technologies community describes itself as an 'online village . . . especially designed to help participants [teachers] clarify their goals, collaborate with others to extend their under-standing, and reflect on their progress and plans' (www.learnwebharvard.edu/ent). Participants have 'backpacks', which include a user profile that allows participants to get to know each other. There is a workshop with tools to help in curriculum design and the production of materials, but the emphasis is on facilitating collaboration in designing, revising and saving jointly developed products.

The Transformational Learning Community (TLC) (www. transform.org) goes beyond this in terms of dialogue. This internet-based resource works towards fundamental change through developing innovative approaches to dialogue and networking. The community promotes dialogue for deeper collective inquiry into thinking processes and into the nature of thought. Dialogue is seen as 'deeply reflective listening and speaking, speaking when truly moved, "suspending" one's assumptions and "noble certainties" by holding them up for examination, and speaking into the group rather than to individuals listening in the silence for the shared flow of meaning' (www.notschool.net; www. learnwebharvard.edu/ent; www.transform.org). Dialogue can open us to a deeper collective inquiry into our own thinking processes and the nature of thought itself.

In addition to dialogue, the TLC has an ethos that values generative thinking (supporting individuals and groups in moving towards more open and creative thought and activity), healthy relationships (based on really knowing the people with whom we collaborate) and authentic needs. They describe themselves as 'an open group of diverse individuals joining in community, learning how to work together, and synergizing our resources and energies to foster positive changes toward more conscious, healthy transformations of ourselves, our communities, and our world'.

It is our understanding that, just like ordinary classrooms and to a lesser extent informal learning situations, electronic learning environments may be motivating and engaging or they may not. What makes for good learning, i.e. what is transformational, meaningful and lifelong, is the attention to aspects of the learning environment and learning process. The new technologies do not solve problems but present new challenges in fostering relationships, communication and participation in new scenarios. The transparency of the fact that no one has the answers as to how to make this work may be in new technology's favour. This may take away some of the threat inherent in ordinary classrooms, it may allow young people to contribute from positions of relative strength and it may allow people to construct themselves and their relationships differently. However enabling new technologies may be, learners still need support and feedback from more experienced others (who may, of course, be other learners rather than teachers) and learning communities still have to be created with the same key principles remaining central.

Language and action

However it is achieved, coming to voice in learning communities returns us to Freire's (1972) radical vision of learners joining with an educator and with one another, to take responsibility for the themes through which they become critically aware and active. Freire gives an example of people who 'verbalize the connection between earning low wages, feeling exploited, and getting drunk – getting drunk as a flight from reality, as an attempt to overcome the frustration of inaction, as an ultimately self-destructive solution' (Freire, 1972, p. 90).

Attempts to take responsibility for one's life – to cease being either oppressor or oppressed – may be linked also to the work of Habermas and the concept of communicative action. How may we live together without domination? How may we come to an understanding of how to live together in community? For Habermas, the answer lies in our human faculty for language, a topic to which we return again and again in this book. Habermas believes that a revival of the public sphere of democratic decision-making requires 'the organization of social communication in a way approximating to an unconstrained dialogue' and 'the development of norms which could fulfil the dialectic of moral relationships in an interaction free of domination' (Outhwaite, 1994, p. 16).

Research in both social psychology and social anthropology shows clearly that human beings are co-operative creatures and that there are universal patterns of human language use and rationality (Harkin, 1998c). When exceptions were found, such as among the Ik of East Africa (Turnbull, 1973), where children had to fend for themselves by the age of 3 and there was no sharing of food, even between spouses, this was seen as a sign of great social distress. The Ik died out. There is far more that unites human beings than divides us and yet everywhere oppression is found – in the family, in schools and colleges and in workplaces, not because we are prone to oppress but because we have constructed oppressive ways of being together. Perhaps it is also because we too are, in a sense, in distress as a society – a distress that may be seen everywhere – not least in the indifference to democratic processes when democracy is reduced to an occasional ballot paper and many young people are disaffected from an education that fails to address their lived experience.

As we have argued, for a different, more communitarian practice of education to become more pervasive, it is necessary to break out of a longstanding equilibrium in which teachers' roles are constructed as active transmitters of knowledge, while learners' roles are constructed as relatively passive recipients of teacher knowledge. It means moving beyond the 'comfort zone' of most present practices, to be open to the challenge of change, based on taking account of multiple and sometimes highly critical perspectives on teaching and learning. Wells (1999) outlines some of the personal skills needed to take part in a new model of work between teachers and learners:

> The skills required to take an exchange from the realm of listening to perspective-taking involve moving from ignoring, through pretending to listen, through partially listening, through active and reflective listening, to empathic listening . . . perspective-taking . . . becomes paramount in maintaining the focus of learning together in a community when the blocks of threatening change, insecurity and obvious differences arise.
>
> (Wells, 1999, p. 133)

We endorse Hoban's (1999) call for teachers engaged in such a fundamental process of professional re-orientation to take part in 'action learning', in which small groups of colleagues meet regularly to help each other improve their practices. This is what happened with Feldman's (1999) Physics teachers discussed in Chapter 7 and in Melanie's example of the way in which

Intensive Interaction evolved. It may be necessary to stimulate this work by opening a conversation with learners, so that they too become part of the action learning as we outline in the example of Joe's research in Chapter 9. These are all very different examples of teachers and/or learners being open and reflective. It is being 'open to inquiry' that Young (1992) calls for in teaching and learning:

> In schooling . . . there will be a lot of instruction, lecturing, reading up and the like. After all, the children have to catch up on several thousand years of inquiry in a few. But open to inquiry means being aware of the processes that produced the knowledge, having some practice in open-ended inquiry for themselves, and/ or awareness of the ongoing inquiry – the contemporary discourse – and some degree of access to that discourse. That means, of course, access to a community.
>
> (Young, 1992, p. 13)

Such openness to inquiry and belonging to a community of learning requires that learners' voices are heard, as well as those of teachers; in a process of critical and rational, evidence-based discourse – which is what critical theory is. Young (1992, p. 16) goes on: 'there is no machinery for cranking out the truth . . . learners cannot acquire true or warranted belief (knowledge) by the application of fixed rules . . . this is not the way that human communities of inquiry learn'. Instead, learners learn by a more hermeneutic process of inquiry, much like the practice of many teachers of literature, in which interpretations are made, defended and refuted and more complex, better understandings arrived at. Learners learn through interactive processes, which, when set in the context of learning communities, means interactions that are unthreatening, meaningful, challenging and enjoyable and thus learning is intrinsically motivating.

Chapter 9

Talking About Communication

In this chapter we return to our central premise that good learning is transformative learning. This takes place in the context of nurturing relationships and open communication between teachers and learners. Re-making education to increase the engagement of learners in a process through which they are empowered to take responsibility for their own learning is happening all over the world as we write. Here, a primary school in England; there, a secondary school in Australia; elsewhere, a university in Japan – all are embarked on similar endeavours to do things differently and to create genuine learning communities. One feature of all these endeavours is the opening of interaction between persons. A learning community, as we have argued, involves people sharing emotional ties, values and beliefs through frequent interaction. Relatively open processes of communication that are as far as possible free from domination are an essential condition of a learning community. In this chapter we look in more detail at interaction and communication styles, drawing in particular on the research of Joe Harkin.

For Habermas (1986), the possibility of community is embedded in our faculty for language:

> The human interest in autonomy and responsibility is not mere fancy . . . what raises us out of nature is the only thing whose nature we can know: language. Through its structure, autonomy and responsibility are posited for us. Our first sentence expresses unequivocally the intention of universal and unconstrained consensus.
>
> (Habermas, 1986, p. 314)

Like Habermas, we hold in high esteem the ability to use language and we regard good communication as essential for good learning. We have some discomfort with equating language use with being human, however, knowing that some learners never develop language. Much of the work of Melanie Nind has addressed ways of working with people who are pre-verbal and often pre-intentional to enhance the communication and inter-action abilities of those learners together with their communication partners. Their humanness is never in question. To foster communication abilities, though, is to foster social inclusion and participation.

In this chapter we focus on more sophisticated language use. We argue that to foster ways in which dialogue is less constrained and interaction is free from domination has many advantages. Many of these have long been recognized. For example, an OECD report stated that

> a large number [of secondary pupils] in all countries lack motivation in school and later fail or under-achieve badly . . . What is now required is a radical re-thinking of this phase of education, taking the adolescent pupils and their views as the point of departure. This will involve widespread changes in curriculum, in personal relations, in assessment, and in guidance and orientation.
>
> (OECD, 1978, p. 25)

If we start with learners and their views, we must also start with ways of listening and hearing those views. Young people, more than ever before, are highly ICT literate and can access knowledge independently through technological sources and libraries. We believe that what is needed is educational settings in which learners can interact with teachers and with one another to learn the human significance of knowledge and, at the same time, to learn about themselves and about difference and tolerance. Education requires more than a Kantian treating of persons as ends in themselves: it requires the affirmation of the person as a person, in a process that balances personal and rational autonomy with the fact that the everyday life of humans is one of co-existence.

To foster good learning we need to enable three key things to happen:

- Learners need to experience a desire to know;
- They need a chance to practise in safety; and
- They need to have sympathetic and positive feedback from someone more 'expert'.

Each of these things involves relationships and communication – reflection and interaction within a supportive framework. The learner needs to be actively engaged at all stages. If the learner is not actively engaged then we have the structure of learning (the institution, the timetable, the curriculum, the assessment regime) but not the change in understanding and/or behaviour which constitutes learning and which fills the structure with human life.

The people with a professional responsibility to fill the structures of education with human life are of course teachers. As Stubbs (1976) put it,

> . . . a person cannot simply walk into a classroom and *be* a teacher: he or she has to *do* quite specific communicative acts . . . social roles such as 'teacher' and 'pupil' do not exist in the abstract. They have to be acted out, performed and continuously constructed in the course of social interaction.
>
> (Stubbs, 1976, p. 99)

Teachers are professional communicators, but they often do their communication work isolated from other teachers and with little feedback about the patterns of interaction they tend to use and whether or to what extent these are effective. There is feedback of course in terms of the non-verbal communications of the participants but teachers are often too focused on other agendas to attune to these fully and respond. Learners may be consulted at the end of a course of study and feedback in informal ways may be gleaned during a learning programme, but detailed and comprehensive sharing of views between teacher and learners about their interaction is rare. One reason for this is that both teachers and learners may lack a vocabulary adequate to explore aspects of interpersonal communication in non-confrontational ways.

Studies of classroom interaction, such as those of Dillon (1994), van Lier (1996) and Ware (1996), have stressed that teachers tend to dominate classroom interaction. This is not altogether the fault of teachers. They work within frameworks of resourcing, curriculum and assessment that constrain what they may do. With fewer such constraints, their re-working of classroom interactions can be more radical, as the early work on Intensive Interaction showed (Nind and Hewett, 1994).

The work of Vygotsky and Bruner, discussed elsewhere in this book, emphasizes the co-construction of knowledge through the interpersonal sharing of understanding, leading to intrapersonal understanding and the internalization of meaning. If it is desirable that learners exercise more control over their own learning in the co-construction of knowledge, as well as developing the capability to be lifelong learners, then a focus upon how teachers tend routinely to interact with their learners is needed. This may provide a stimulus for reflection by teachers about how we might develop our repertoire of teaching strategies and promote more autonomous and therefore good learning. As teachers we need (1) to understand the nature of language and communication and (2) to be enabled to reflect critically and positively on how we tend routinely to interact with learners.

The social purposes of language

A characteristic of humans who have gone through typical development is a highly evolved ability to use language. According to Aitchison (1996), this may have evolved from grooming behaviour. Once primate groups exceeded about 150 individuals mutual grooming was insufficient to bond the group together and language may have developed as a means of extending grooming behaviour – which is more about social bonding than cleansing. The importance of language use in social bonding is exemplified every day throughout the world. 'Good morning', 'Fine weather', 'How are you?' are the sorts of routine greetings that people use to establish or maintain contact with others. It may not be a 'good' morning; the weather may be dull; and the question may not really be meant to elicit a response about a person's health or state of mind. These are examples of what the anthropologist Malinowski (1935) called 'phatic communion' – language used to overcome silence and interact with others. Classrooms and other learning environments need some of this phatic communion if they are to foster effective social connections between participants in the learning endeavour.

Learning communities, as we saw in the last chapter, are possible only when all participants – learners as well as teachers – have a voice. It is necessary for them to be able to express their point of view, listen and respond sensitively to others and work together to learn. Interaction between teachers and learners is often through spoken language, and spoken language, as we argued in Chapter 4, is fundamentally orientated towards social interaction.

There are, of course, many purposes for language use, from the social to the narrowly transactional to the poetic and self-referential. Popper (1972, pp. 119–20), saw language use in a hierarchy from expressive language at the bottom (shared with bees and other creatures) through to argumentative language, such as philosophizing. Britton (1970) favoured a tripartite division of language into transactional–expressive–poetic, with the poetic viewed as the most sophisticated. We are less concerned here with the relative sophistication of different forms of language use and more concerned with the way we can use language and communication for good learning and in learning communities.

Teachers' critical reflection on communication with learners

Interactions between teachers and learners are influenced by many factors beyond teachers' control. These make it all the more important that we avoid facile judgements, from a position of being outsiders, about 'right' or 'wrong' styles of teacher communication. Communication and interaction are maintained through continual negotiation by participants. Moreover, they are to a large extent culture- and situation-specific. As we saw in the early models of communication development discussed in Chapter 2, however, there are principles about optimal communicating that we can use to guide us.

Whenever there are more two or more people in a conversation, a relationship is established. The relationship may, of course, exist only as a feature of that individual conversation or it may be extended over a significant time frame. The relationship may be more or less warm; and one person may exert more or less control over the relationship than the other. Tnese two factors, *warmth* and *control*, shape the nature of the interaction between people (Leary, 1957). Different writers have used different terms for this fundamental juxtaposition of factors; for example Brown (1986) refers to *status* and *solidarity* and Dunkin and Biddle (1974) refer to *directivity* and *warmth*. The Oxford Brookes *Communication Styles* project (Harkin *et al.*, 1999) adopted the terms *warmth* and *control* because they could be understood readily by young adult learners.

The combination of a degree of warmth and a degree of control in interpersonal communication is present in all situations, whether social, in business or education, whether children or adults are involved or whether the situation is formal or casual. Spoken communication in the classroom tends to be a formalized, conventional encounter in which teachers are expected to exercise relatively high levels of control; nevertheless, the normal conventions of human interaction are not suspended altogether. Warmth and control are, of course, exhibited by more than spoken language – we can say one thing but do another and establish particular kinds of relationships with others in many other ways than in our use of spoken language. 'Warmth' and 'control' form part of an overall pattern of behaviour or style of interaction in particular situations. We may be hostile to colleagues and warm to family or we may be a warm and supportive teacher with one group of learners but less so with another. Furthermore, in interaction we are not free to establish unilaterally the nature of the relationship. As we saw in Chapter 2, this is reciprocal and transactional and even young babies are co-determiners of patterns of interpersonal relations.

Every teacher knows that learners help determine patterns of classroom interaction.

Drawing on the work over many years of Wubbels (Wubbels and Levy, 1993), Brekelmans (1989) and others at the University of Utrecht, researchers at Oxford Brookes University developed a *Communication Styles Questionnaire* (CSQ), designed as a tool to help teachers reflect on how they tend to communicate with young adult learners. The questionnaire provides teachers who wish to have more detailed feedback about their communication with students with a means to obtain this in a valid and reliable way. It may also help develop a vocabulary that teachers and learners together may use to discuss classroom interaction, which may also promote greater mutual understanding and collaboration between teachers and learners.

The development and validation of the CSQ is documented in Harkin *et al.* (1999). Each question in the CSQ provides data for one of eight contrasting scales of measurement of the teacher–learner interaction. These give rise to scale scores, as well as individual item scores showing teacher perceptions and student perceptions of classroom interaction, based on actual interaction and perceptions of ideal interaction. For ease of joint discussion with students, the data may also be presented in outline in octagons (Figure 9.1). The information may then be used by the teachers to reflect on patterns of teacher–learner interaction and, if thought appropriate by the teacher (we believe that it is always appropriate), students may be engaged in discussion with the teacher about the implications of the results for the way that they work together in learning. Following this reflection and discussion, action may be taken to bring about change towards more positive and beneficial patterns of interaction. The action may be by the teacher and the students.

Analysis of data from 75 teachers and more than 1000 learners in 6 further education colleges and school sixth forms (Harkin and Davis, 1996) showed that 'warmth' is perceived as more important than 'control' as a factor in teacher–student relationships in post-compulsory education, particularly in vocational education. This was corroborated by subsequent studies of the constructs that students use when informally evaluating their

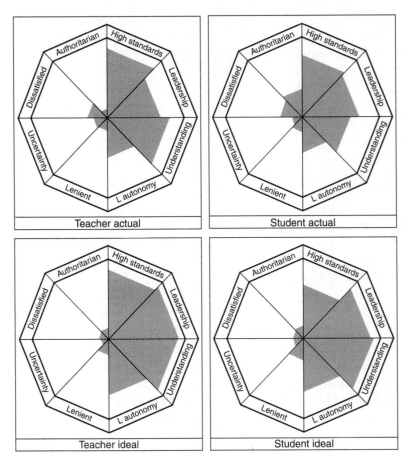

Figure 9.1   Teacher–learner interaction

teachers in Norway (Johannessen *et al.*, 1997) and England (Harkin, 1998b). These studies show that education, even of young adults who are focused on instrumental goals, such as gaining vocational qualifications or entry to university, is an experience in which knowledge is not simply transmitted, but in which human relationships are immensely important to learning. This refers both to relationships to create a suitable climate for learning and relationships involved in overcoming the difficulties of one person 'transmitting' through language anything of value to another. For learning to happen, people need to relate to others; to converse; to speak for themselves; and to internalize the new knowledge in their own language.

'Warmth' in education is far from a 'touchy-feely' experience. It is not the same as friendship or counselling. It is establishing a perception among learners that they are valued as individuals and supported in their learning goals. It is closely bound up with the concept of 'leadership' and a perception that a teacher understands the subject or learning content and its assessment and is able to shape learning to meet the needs of *these* individual learners.

The 'warmth' factor in interaction may be subdivided into two contrasting sets of behaviours:

Leadership in contrast to *uncertainty*
Understanding in contrast to *dissatisfaction.*

Table 9.1 describes some of the characteristics of typical teacher behaviour on the 'warmth' dimension of human inter-action. It shows that what we say and how we listen to others are important, but so too are many non-verbal behaviours, such as how much time we devote to others, how engaged we are in tasks, how knowledgeable and committed we are and so on.

Similarly, the 'control' factor in interaction may be subdivided into two contrasting sets of behaviours:

Authoritarianism in contrast to *learner autonomy*
High standards in contrast to *leniency.*

Table 9.2 describes some of the characteristics of typical teacher behaviour on the 'control' dimension of human interac-tion. It may be seen that it is possible to control others either by exerting power and authority – and as Lear said, 'a dog's obeyed in office' – or by setting high standards that you yourself demonstrate.

The development of a 'science' for education, as advocated by Carr (1995), drawing on Habermas, is linked closely to the idea of reconstructing the experience of education in a critical dia-

Table 9.1   Warmth dimension

Dissatisfaction e.g. teacher:	*Leadership e.g. teacher:*
Displays a pessimistic view of students as people who are unable to act responsibly or to learn successfully.	Appears to be a dependable, 'safe' pair of hands.
	Understands the subject and its assessment.
Takes little or no interest in students as individual persons.	Designs learning activities with a particular group of students in mind.
Is heavy-handed in criticism, undermining learner self-confidence.	Is prepared to change tack and vary activities to enhance learning by, for example, drawing on learner experience and interest.
Is prone to sarcasm and/or anger.	
Instils a negative opinion of learner potential.	Is confident enough to share jokes and humour with students.
	Instils respect for the teacher.
Uncertainty e.g. teacher:	*Understanding e.g. teacher:*
Appears to be undependable.	Displays an optimistic view of students as people who are capable of acting responsibly and of learning successfully.
Appears unsure of the subject and/of the assessment requirements.	
Displays a weak grasp of the learning needs of a particular group of students.	Knows individual students by name.
	Monitors individual performance and gives help when needed.
Instils disrespect for the teacher.	Takes an interest in students beyond their role as learners.
	Instils self-respect and confidence in learners.

logue among teachers. We argue that learners too, of almost all ages and abilities, should be brought actively into the discussion, not simply to corroborate the views of others but to introduce their own perceptions. The rational reconstruction of action to

Table 9.2 Control dimension

Authoritarianism e.g. teacher:	*High standards e.g. teacher:*
Prefers students to be quiet and passive, to listen and take notes.	Is punctual.
Dominates interaction, even during discussions.	Is well prepared to teach.
	Has high expectations of student effort and performance.
Uses assessment to control and motivate.	Is fair in assessing against criteria and gives useful, critical feedback.
Instils fear.	*Instils respect for learning.*
Leniency e.g. teacher:	*Learner autonomy e.g. teacher:*
May not be punctual.	Encourages students to play an active role in learning by, for example, consulting them about activities, setting work that challenges them to find out for themselves and to solve real-life problems.
Is not well prepared to teach.	
Has low expectations of student effort and performance.	
Is lenient in assessment, passing poor quality work.	Encourages student–student as well as teacher–student interaction.
Fails to control student behaviour and may abdicate responsibility for this.	Uses self and peer assessment to help learners understand what they know and still need to learn.
Instils lack of respect for learning.	*Instils responsibility.*

improve know-how in Habermas's (1987) opinion rarely leads to change, unless it incorporates reflection as critical insight into the distortions built into participants' reconstructions of action. This is possible only if teachers have a framework to guide this process even if subsequently it is no longer needed. The CSQ is designed to provide such a framework for self-directed professional development, based on critical self-reflection. Importantly, it allows the possibility of opening a discussion with learners of habitual practices of interaction, based on clear evidence of different perceptions.

An example of the use of the CSQ illustrates the process of teacher reflection and self-directed professional development. A lecturer in Accounting was unhappy with the opportunities for students to develop their own learning and used the CSQ to compare his students' views with his own. The CSQ results showed that the lecturer and the students perceived the current experience offered very limited learner autonomy and that both sets of participants wanted to see this element increased. The lecturer, therefore, held a discussion with the students and as a result discovered that they particularly wanted more choice in what they studied and the opportunity to choose the assignments they worked on. With this in mind, the lecturer planned and ran a new module in Accounting expressly to stimulate learner autonomy, to develop initiative in learning and to motivate students to better results. Features of the module included:

- encouraging students to use their initiative through contributing suggestions for alternative or additional syllabus content;
- giving students greater control over their learning experience through allowing each student to set his or her own topic and essay title for the assessed coursework;
- encouraging students to use each other as resources and potential sources of guidance rather than relying solely on the lecturer;
- ensuring that students carried out research for class sessions on which class discussions were subsequently held.

The lecturer monitored and reflected on the impact of the module on his students' experience as it progressed and after it had finished. The CSQ was once again completed by the lecturer and by the new group of students and showed that learner perceptions of the degree of their autonomy had increased and that he was moving towards his ideal model of communication with these students.

The lecturer's actions, in developing more student–student interaction and in creating the conditions for greater learner autonomy, reveal that teachers can change the nature of their interactions with learners. This is a powerful fact and one that goes to the heart of what it means to be a 'professional', engaged in 'evidence-based practice'. If these terms are to mean something worthwhile, rather than be empty rhetoric, then we need to reflect critically but positively upon how we tend to work with learners and to take any steps we consider necessary to develop that relationship.

Extending the principle of reflection on interaction

Here it is important to recognize that learners have something positive and worthwhile to contribute in determining how they are taught and how they learn. Learners regarded as of generally low ability and as displaying 'behavioural difficulties' at times show themselves capable of making sensitive and considered judgements about teaching and learning and, given the right conditions, normally and routinely make such judgements (Hockley and Harkin, 2000). The 'right' conditions are neither rare nor difficult to create, they simply involve making plain to learners that their views are valued and will be taken seriously, together with sharing with them a common vocabulary (such as that provided by the CSQ) for discussing classroom interaction in 'objective', non-confrontational ways.

In Britain, which prides itself on its democracy, the views of learners about what they learn, how they learn and when they learn are rarely considered. Teachers too are rarely consulted about teaching and learning processes or given opportunities to take stock of how they tend to teach. Few schools and colleges in the UK have heard of the Organizing Bureau of European School Student Unions (OBESSU) (discussed in Chapter 8), despite the existence of this EU-funded organization for many years. There is not a tradition of open discussion between teachers and learners of the joint enterprise in which they are engaged.

The communication styles of teachers should encourage more democratic participation in the process of learning and teaching. This may be accomplished without difficulty in most learning situations if the will exists. A beginning point for more democratic and participative education is for teachers to take stock from time to time of how they tend routinely and habitually to interact with learners. The project we have used as an extended example in this chapter has been concerned with students in further or higher education, but similar vehicles are available for guiding reflection on different kinds of interactions. Melanie Nind has used a self-appraisal framework adapted from a parent-coaching programme (Clark and Seifer, 1983) for use in a similar process but by teachers of pupils with severe and complex learning difficulties. The framework can be used to reflect on interactions in a teacher's mind's eye or on video. It similarly focuses on routine interactions with learners and asks, for example, 'Am I regularly . . .

- uninvolved? – mechanical in my interactions with little eye contact or smiling
- forcing? – demanding in my interactions . . .
- 'overriding? – intrusive in my interactions, interrupting the flow of the person's activity with a requirement for a different behaviour or activity
- involved? – responsive . . .
- acknowledging? . . .
- [through to]
- engaging? – responsive in a way that builds on knowledge of the person and of how to engage them for extended periods.
                                        (Nind and Hewett, 2001, p. 109)

The willingness to take stock of how one tends routinely to interact should be applied across the whole educational community including nurseries and pre-school provision. It should also be extended to include education managers, addressing their interactions with teachers, parents and others. A culture of open and participative education, as a joint enterprise between learners and teachers, cannot exist if the host culture of educational institutions does not display democratic processes.

Sharing of control over learning inevitably involves some cognitive and affective conflict; no human relationships can proceed without conflict and the extent to which conflict is discussed openly so that people can come to understandings of the situation is a mark of the health of those relationships. By their mutually determined roles, however, teachers and students rarely come into conflict in 'well-ordered' classrooms. Rather than share control and risk conflict we tend to structure and manage interaction by selecting 'problems' to be discussed or tasks to be 'solved'. 'The only context in which children can reverse interactional roles with the same intellectual content, giving directions as well as following them, and asking questions as well as answering them, is with peers' (Forman and Cazden, 1998, p. 204).

We have discussed the roles of peers in collaborative learning in Chapter 7 and we know that the affective support of a friend helps in learning complex new knowledge (Azmitia, 1998). This corroborates the evidence from the CSQ, Quali-teach and Intensive Interaction projects outlined in this book about the fundamental importance of human warmth in learning. In this chapter we have looked at teachers' communication and inter-action styles and at structured ways of enhancing these. It is important to remember, though, that however skilled the teacher and however willing to share control, teachers cannot be other than teachers. Peers offer something quite different and, as teachers and as participants in learning communities, we must facilitate peer interaction and learning as much as focus on our own development and interactions with learners.

Chapter 10

A Manifesto for Learning

In this concluding chapter we restate the principles of good learning that have underpinned the earlier chapters. We discuss our growing belief that these principles are both fundamental and universal. We then go on to explore some of the practical challenges that we, as teachers, face in applying these principles in the current climate. Finally, we look forward.

Fundamental Principles

Throughout this book we have asserted that good learning should be

- transformative
- active and interactive
- intrinsically motivating and
- lifelong

and that it takes place in the context of

- nurturing relationships and
- rich communications.

In the first instance these principles emerged from and informed our individual teaching, often helped by theorists, fellow practitioners and learners. Later the principles were consolidated for us as we conducted our separate research. Throughout our research they have been central to our research questions, chosen methodologies and preferred modes of dissemination. The principles have a continuing influence on our thinking, not least about the principles themselves.

As we, the authors, collaborated together we came to a deeper understanding of the principles and their centrality in all our work. By exploring their application within our different professional contexts we have become convinced of their relevance to our work in infant, primary, secondary, special, further and higher education.

During the process of writing this book we have become increasingly convinced of both the soundness of the principles and of their universality. We recognize that these principles can be difficult to apply, especially in the current climate where counter-messages dominate. How well we apply principles depends often on factors we see as beyond our control. Consequently, there is inconsistency and there is both good and not so good practice in our educational institutions. This is reflected in our following discussion of practice within the current climate.

The current climate

People are hardwired for learning and from the earliest age learn the most complex things with ease. The process of caregiver interaction with an infant shows the importance to learning of nurturing relationships, reciprocal communication, active participation and of mutual fun, which become the nutrients for further learning. However, formal educational institutions often have climates and practices that get in the way of learning. Despite the many successes of formal education, which should not be ignored – many people in the world desire our abundance of education, just as they desire our abundance of food or cars – the plain fact is that many young people are deeply alienated from it. Many learn little that they value highly; and many of those who 'succeed' and go on to higher education may regard the process as a tedious treadmill only justified by the long-term goal of a secure, professional job. For many teachers and learners there is little intrinsic joy in the process of education. We have constructed ways of being together in formal education that are dull, draining of human creativity, and that fly in the face of intrinsically motivating learning.

There is a normalcy in our society that may be characterized as individualistic consumerism and unsurprisingly formal education has been constructed as a pattern or microcosm of this normalcy. The normative goal that drives the whole of education is academic qualifications awarded to the minority at the end of formal education. Whilst the acquisition of this product is a reality for some, it acts as a means of excluding and constructing as other all those for whom it is an irrelevance.

In the present situation in England and Wales, students who drop out of extrinsically motivated courses effectively drop out of formalized learning, unless they are rescued by a remedial programme such as vocational access courses in colleges of further education. Alternatively, they may be given mentor support through the Connexions service (affection for the disaffected); or possibly, if they are one of the lucky few, put on an experimental programme, such as www.notschool.net, where again they will be given one-to-one support to learn. Like prisons or taking children into care, these programmes are costly remediation for deep-seated problems that it would be more fruitful and far cheaper to tackle earlier.

Despite a minimal head-nodding towards religion and to citizenship, the values and beliefs that drive education provision are rooted in individual consumption of goods and services. In this regard, nothing has changed since Matthew Arnold wrote in 1863 about the Philistines (English middle classes) who are

> of all people the most inaccessible to ideas and the most impatient of them; inaccesible to them, because of their want of familarity with them; and impatient of them because they have got on so well without them, that they despise those who, not having got on so well as themselves, still make a fuss for what they themselves have done so well without.
>
> (Arnold, 1863, p. 140)

An education system without guiding values and beliefs beyond the pragmatic soon gets lost in a time when, according to Giddens (1991), life in modernity may be experienced as a juggernaut, 'a runaway engine of enormous power which, collectively as human beings, we can drive to some extent but which also threatens to rush out of our control' (p. 139).

Formal education may be seen to deal relatively effectively with the easy tasks – teaching well-codified, public knowledge to individuals who are motivated by longer-term extrinsic goals, in ways that can be readily assessed. It does not deal well with more complex areas of 'real' human knowledge; nor with individuals who are not so well motivated by extrinsic goals; nor with knowledge that is not readily assessed. Formal education is fragmenting and disintegrating as knowledge becomes more complex; as individuals become more dissatisfied with normal provision and want education to meet intrinsic needs; and as the burdens of individualized assessment become heavier and less tenable by learners and teachers.

In the present situation, traditional schooling does not offer an adequate affective environment for many individuals. The environment lacks opportunities for rich communication within nurturing relationships. Furthermore, traditional schooling does not chime with the nature of learners' lives; their interests; their aspirations. It does not offer enough personally meaningful challenges or enough security in which to take risks without losing face. For many young people, schooling is not only a dreary and irrelevant experience but also a threatening one. Schooling challenges the life styles, beliefs, ideals and consequently the very identities of many learners.

The work of Vygotsky and of those like Bruner and Salmon who have developed his ideas shows clearly how education can be different and how people learn through collaboration with others, in the pursuit of personally meaningful goals. People need other people to learn in an intrinsically motivating, social process in which challenges are faced, mistakes made, helpful feedback given and new attempts made leading to success. In this active process, the journey is as important as the outcomes or goals, for goals once reached simply become the starting point for new journeys. As Cavafy (1978) wrote,

> You must always have Ithaka in your mind,
> Arrival there is your predestination.
> But do not hurry the journey at all.
> Better that it should last many years;
> Be quite old when you anchor at the island,
> Rich with all you have gained on the way,
> Not expecting Ithaka to give you riches.
> Ithaka has given you your lovely journey.

If lifelong learning is to mean anything beyond the hollow notion that it is learning that takes place after formal schooling, it is that learning is potentially a wonderful journey through the rich complexities of human knowledge, with an abundance and a variety to suit all tastes. It is not outcomes that matter – they are provisional, arbitrary, often foolish and unsatisfactory – but the journey itself. Despite the way they are often presented within the current climate, teachers are not technicians of outcomes, but guides to journeys All journeys begin necessarily with where we are and not from an alternative starting point that would make the journey easier! If young people are expected to start out from nowhere they recognize, then for many the journey does not even begin. Frustrated, they will rebel, doze or drop out, depending on their temperament and the influence of those around them.

The learning journey begins, then, with individual choice, prompted by others who care – whether as parents or as teachers. It begins with the life-world of each unique individual and must necessarily offer real participation in personally meaningful activities. This is far different from the specious 'teamwork' or 'assignments' of many current courses that keep young people busy but teach them little or nothing. Such 'busywork' occupies time and helps to control dissidence. As Bates (1998) pointed out, students become 'hunters and gatherers' of often personally meaningless information, to be recorded tediously in ever fattening portfolios of evidence or lifelong learning logs. This may keep youth off the streets, but it is unlikely to teach them anything that they believe to be worthwhile or turn them into lifelong learners.

The remedy is to found education upon the real lives of young people and to begin the journey from where they are. This amounts to a form of democratization of education because, in order to begin where individuals are, you have to listen to them; having listened you then have to respond appropriately. In this way education becomes transformative. This turns on its head the present model of education in which teachers, as representatives of a bureaucracy, first determine what people will learn and then present them with a specification of the outcomes they must achieve. Pre-set outcomes; to be reached at pre-determined times, will inevitably miss the mark for many people – for some the goal is too trivial and dull; for others too challenging so that they are labelled failures almost from the outset. It also sets up an aggressive model of education in which there will be 'winners' who can reach the pre-set finishing line in the time set and 'losers' who fail to achieve this. As Goffmann (1956), Collins (1996) and others have shown, people avoid loss of face at all costs – rather than being educational 'losers' they will simply not enter the race; alternatively, they triumph as bullies or find other ways of gaining respect.

Many schools and colleges do not apply what we would see as fundamental principles of good learning and have become dysfunctional communities of practice. A community has shared norms and dysfunctional communities display dysfunctional norms: teachers who are constrained to behave in ways that they may find personally harmful or even offensive, and learners constrained to be or to become persons that are offensive. Teachers may become aggressive authority figures who place major effort into controlling young people's behaviour. Alternatively, they may become technicians of subject matter and assessment regimes in which they have no personal belief. Or they may abdicate responsibility for learning to spurious 'learner-centred' approaches that amount to little more than 'go away and find out for yourselves'. Similarly, young people may become passive recipients of information that may mean little or nothing to them; or strategists of assessment regimes who do whatever they need to get through and get out; or cynical failures who regard anyone who studies as a contemptible swot. As communities are interactive, equilibria are established in which one set of teacher or student behaviours reinforces corresponding behaviours. We end up with stable but dysfunctional equilibria and, in England at least, given a propensity for pragmatic tinkering rather than more thorough and principled thinking, it is assumed that this is the way the world is and that nothing can be done to improve ways of being together in education.

There is, then, a sense in which there is a great deal of co-operation in present formal education. Teachers and students co-operate in dysfunctional equilibria. What they often do not do in the present state of affairs is collaborate. Collaboration between teachers and learners and between learners themselves is rare in education. Collaboration requires communication within relationships, which results in shared power and shared responsibility. Collaboration requires people working *together* in the pursuit of common goals that they value.

In order to promote collaborative learning, teachers need to establish a learning climate that produces collaboration. As in ecology, climates give rise to certain forms of growth; conversely, they make other forms of growth impossible. While collaboration implies a necessity to share power, it remains true to say that teachers will always have more power in an asymmetrical relationship with learners. It is part of teachers' professionalism to create a suitable climate for collaborative learning. The key to accomplishing it is the application of our principles.

These principles require us, as teachers, to *like* the learners and *care* about their welfare; to *listen* to them and *respond* to what they have to say. Teaching and learning, for all participants, is an *emotional* activity, as has been recognized by each of us individually through our research and experience and by others, such as Nias (1996) and Hargreaves (1998). An application of the principles necessitates that it is the *process* of education that is highlighted and not learning outcomes. The outcomes will follow if the process is healthy; the growth will occur if the climate is conducive.

Clearly, there are serious constraints upon any teacher's ability to act in the ways described. Constraints of curriculum, assessment, resourcing, class sizes, time, expectations. Some of these constraints, especially many assessment regimes, are formidable barriers to ways of working suited to good learning and instead promote individual and aggressive surface learning. Education managers and policy-makers have a great responsibility in creating and maintaining conditions that are inimical to genuine learner participation and worthwhile, lifelong learning.

The distinction between the 'effective' school and the 'person-centred' school (Fielding, 1999) is a useful one in reinforcing our principles. Many schools and colleges are highly effective institutions in terms of league tables and other outcome measures. However, it does not automatically follow that they are happy places or that the learning is personally meaningful to students or 'deep' and able to be transferred to learners' lives beyond formal education. The Fryer Report (1997) on lifelong learning recommended that

> The focus of policy and practice should be learners themselves . . .
> This would shift attention away from structures and institutions,
> which should be regarded as more or less efficient mechanisms for
> the delivery of demonstrably high quality learning.
>
> (Fryer, 1997, p. 29)

This is not to deny that there may be a close relationship between good management and good learning, but rather to assert that the former cannot be judged without reference to the latter. Much of the inclusive education movement is about a radical redesign of schools rather that a focus on individual learners' deficits (Ballard, 1995; Stainback and Stainback, 1996). This is a move to make schools more learner-centred, to adapt them to diverse learners rather than having to adapt learners to them. Thus there is a simultaneous concern for systems and for learners, but with active participation and quality of commitment of teachers and learners as central. We believe that by grasping our principles and acting on them, teachers can improve the quality of learning throughout education.

The way forward

To ensure good learning, clear principles and ideal models must be held in mind and practised. Pragmatism is never, ever enough. This book has drawn on the work of people such as Paulo Freire, bell hooks, Jurgen Habermas and Thomas Sergiovanni, to indicate the shape of possible learning futures. Freire argues for education to be based on an authentic dialogue between teachers and learners. hooks asserts a need for excitement in learning generated by collective effort. Habermas calls for an unconstrained dialogue between people that may lead to reaching consensus without domination. Sergiovanni helps to articulate the properties of authentic learning communities in which people can collaborate in the pursuit of shared and personally meaningful goals.

All these writers, in different ways, point to the vital importance of language use within education. The normal forms of language use in a civilized society often break down in present educational practice: the Gricean (1975) maxims of speaking truthfully and sincerely and of turn-taking; and Lakoff's (1977) principle of politeness. If people talked to each other outside as they often talk to each other within education, there would be little possibility of human collaboration. The English Parliament, with the unedifying spectacle of highly educated, middle-class people shouting each other down, is a disgraceful example to all young people. It is ironic that most politicians are perfectly polite outside the chamber – even to each other – and have control of the shaping of the education system.

No educational system nor educational institution nor subject area nor classroom topic should be practised without a firm bedrock of values and beliefs. Noddings (1996) holds that for 200 years we have avoided admitting how important affect is in education (and in other areas of life) but that

> all students seek connections – connections among the subjects
> they are forced to study, connections to their concrete life
> situations and connections to the great existential questions. If this
> is true, then teachers might try to enhance their own affective

responses by looking at their subjects in terms of these
connections.

(Noddings, 1996, p. 442)

We endorse the view of Sergiovanni and Starrat (1988) that
values and beliefs are at the heart of all cultural activities. We
either articulate the values and beliefs that we wish to inform
our practice; or, unacknowledged, we base our practice on values
and beliefs that may lead us to grief. Ways of working together
have been erected that value individual aggression, reason without affect and consumption, so that even knowledge is viewed as
one more commodity. Instead, we should value the uniqueness
of individual persons, collaboration in community and the sharing of learning journeys.

As teachers we need to reflect critically, with others, on
current practices and why they are so dysfunctional for so many
people. Critical reflection is, however, not easy. We are caught
up as actors in the present situation and need new perspectives.
Perspective taking may begin, importantly, with listening to the
voices of learners telling us about their experiences of life and
education. In most education, the voices of learners have always
been marginal and there is deep distrust that they have anything
constructive to say.

Based on our recent collaboration with each other and with
other teachers, we are reassured that practice is all the time
being changed and enhanced as a result of critical reflection. If
we as teachers can unite behind principled thinking, this reflection has the power to stem the worst excesses of the current
product-driven climate. All learners stand to benefit.

References

Ainscow, M. (1995) 'Education for all: making it happen', *Support for Learning*, **10** (4), 147–55.

Ainscow, M. (1999) *Understanding and Development of Inclusive Schools*. London: Falmer.

Aitchison, J. (1996) *The Seeds of Speech*. Cambridge: Cambridge University Press.

ALBSU (1995) *Parents and their Children: The Intergenerational Effect of Poor Basic Skills*. London: ALBSU.

Alexander, R., Willcocks, J. and Nelson, N. (1996) 'Discourse, pedagogy and the National Curriculum: change and continuity in primary schools', *Research Papers in Education*, **11** (1), 81–120.

Anning, A. (1998) 'Appropriateness or effectiveness in the early childhood curriculum in the UK: some research evidence', *International Journal of Early Years Education*, **6** (3), 299–314.

Arnold, M. (1863) 'Essays in criticism: Philistines', in E. K. Chambers (1954) *Arnold: Poetry and Prose*. Oxford: Clarendon.

Azmitia, M. (1998) 'Peer interactive minds: developmental, theoretical, and methodological issues', in D. Faulkner, K. Littleton and M. Woodhead (eds) *Learning Relationships in the Classroom*. London: Routledge/Open University Press.

Ball, S. (1994) *Start Right: The Importance of Early Learning*. London: Royal Society for the Encouragement of the Arts, Manufacturers and Commerce.

Ballard, K. (1995) 'Inclusion, paradigms, power and participation', in C. Clark, A. Dyson and A. Millward (eds) *Towards Inclusive Schools?* London: David Fulton, pp. 1–14.

Barber, M. (1994) Young People and Their Attitudes to School: An Interim Report of a Research Project in the Centre for Successful Schools. Keele University.

Barnes, D. (1979) *From Communication to Curriculum*. Harmondsworth: Penguin.

Barrett M. and Trevitt, J. (1991) *Attachment Behaviour and the Schoolchild.* London: Routledge.

Bates, I. (1998) 'Resisting 'empowerment' and realizing power: an exploration of aspects of the GNVQ', *Journal of Education and Work,* **11** (2), 187–204.

Bateson, M. C. (1979) 'The epigenesis of conversational interaction', in M. Bullowa (ed.) *Before Speech: The Beginning of Interpersonal Communication.* Cambridge: Cambridge University Press.

Batten, M. (1989) 'Teacher and pupil perspectives on the positive aspects of classroom experience', *Scottish Educational Review,* **21** (1), 48–57.

Bell, R. Q. (1968) 'A reinterpretation of the direction of effects in studies of socialization', *Psychological Review,* **75**, 81–95.

Bellis, A. and Awar, S. (1995) 'Come back when you've learnt some English: refugees, interpreters and teaching ESOL', in Stuart and Thomson (1995).

Bereiter, C. (1998) 'Situated cognition and how to overcome it', in D. Kirshner and J. A. Whitson (eds) *Situated Cognition: Social, Semiotic and Psychological Perspectives.* New York: Lawrence Erlbaum Associates.

Beveridge, S. (1989) 'Parents as teachers of children with special educational needs', in D. Sugden (ed.) *Cognitive Approaches in Special Education.* London: Falmer.

Beveridge, S. (1993) *Special Educational Needs in Schools.* London: Routledge.

Blenkin, G. M. and Kelly, V. (1993) 'Never mind the quality: feel the breadth and balance', in: R. J. Campbell (ed.) *Breadth and Balance in the Primary Curriculum.* London: Falmer.

Bliss, J., Askew, M. and Macrae, S. (1996) 'Effective teaching and learning: scaffolding revisited', *Oxford Review of Education,* **22** (1), 37–61.

Brekelmans, M. (1989) *Interpersonal Teacher Behaviour in the Classroom.* Utrecht: WCC.

Britton, J. (1970) *Prospect and Retrospect.* London: Heinemann.

Brown, R. (1986) *Social Psychology.* London: Collier-Macmillan.

Brufee, K. A. (1994) 'Making the most of knowledgable peers', *Change,* **26** (3), 39–45.

Bruner, J. (1963) 'Needed: a theory of instruction', *Educational Leadership,* **20**, 523–32.

Bruner, J. (1983) *Child's Talk: Learning to Use Language.* New York: Oxford University Press.

Bruner, J. (1996) *The Culture of Education*. London: Harvard University Press.

Bunning, K. (1995) 'Facilitated communication: what are the risks', *Royal College of Speech and Language Therapy Bulletin*, **522**, 9–10.

Burford, B. (1986) 'Communication through movement', in M. Bullowa (ed.) *Before Speech*. Cambridge: Cambridge University Press.

Burhans, K. K. and Dweck, C. S. (1995) 'Helplessness in early childhood: the role of contingent worth', *Child Development*, **66**, 1719–38.

Burnes, R. B. (1979) *The Self-Concept: Theory, Measurement, Development and Behaviour*. London: Longman.

Calhoun, M. L. and Rose, T. L. (1988) 'Early social reciprocity interventions for infants with severe retardation: current findings and implications for the future', *Education and Training in Mental Retardation*, **23**, 340–43.

Carlson, L. and Bricker, D. D. (1982) 'Dyadic and contingent aspects of early communicative intervention', in D. D. Bricker (ed.) *Interventions with At-Risk and Handicapped Infants*. Baltimore: University Park Press.

Carr, W. (1995) *For Education*. Buckingham: Open University Press.

Carr, W. and Hartnett, A. (1996) *Education in the Struggle for Democracy*. Buckingham: Open University Press.

Carrington, S. (1999) 'Inclusion needs a different school culture', *International Journal of Inclusive Education*, **3** (3), 257–68.

Cavafy, C. P. (1978) *Poems Translated by John Mavrogordato*. London: Chatto & Windus.

Cazden, C. (1988) *Classroom Discourse*. London, Heinemann.

Chamberlain, B., Hopper, V. and Jack, B. (1996) *Starting out the Multiple Intelligence Way: A Guide to Multiple Intelligence in Primary School*. Bolton: D2.

Chodorow, N. (1978) *The Reproduction of Mothering*. London: University of California Press.

Cicogani, E. and Zani, B. (1992) 'Teacher–children interaction in a nursery school: an exploratory study', *Language and Education*, **6** (1), 1–12.

Clark, G. N. and Seifer, R. (1983) 'Facilitating mother–infant communication: a treatment model for high-risk and developmentally delayed infants', *Infant Mental Health*, **4** (2), 67–82.

Cleves School staff and pupils, with Priscilla Alderson (1999) *Learning and Inclusion: The Cleves School Experience*. London: David Fulton.

Cochran-Smith, M. and Lytle, S. (1993) *Inside/Outside: Teacher Researcher and Knowledge*. New York: Teachers College Press.

Collins, J. (1993) 'The classroom teacher's use of talk as therapy : the special needs of excessively quiet pupils', in I. L. Gomneas and E. Osborne (eds) *Making Links: How Children Learn*. Norway: Yrkeslitteratur.

Collins, J. (1994) The Silent Minority: Developing Talk in the Primary Classroom. Unpublished PhD thesis, University of Sheffield.

Collins, J. (1996) *The Quiet Child*. London: Cassell.

Collins, J. (1997) Barriers to Communication in Schools. Unpublished paper, BERA, University of York.

Collins, J. (2000a) 'Are you talking to me?: the need to respect and develop a pupil's self image', *Educational Research*, **42** (2), 157–66.

Collins, J. (2000b) 'Exclusion within: a silent protest', in G. Walraven, C. Parsons, D. van Veen, C. Day and C. Garant (eds) *Combating Social Exclusion through Education*. Levedon: Garant.

Collins, J. and Marshall, T. (2001) 'Teaching the Literacy Strategy: a teacher's perspective', *Education 3–13*, **29** (2), 7–12.

Collins, J. and Syred-Paul, A. (1997) 'Children as researchers using CD-ROM', in R. Wegerif and P. Scrimshaw (eds) *Computers and Talk in the Primary Classroom*. London: Routledge.

Collins, J., Littleton, K., Mercer, N,. Scrimshaw, P. and Wegerif, R. (1995) *CD-ROMS in Primary Schools: An Independent Evaluation*. Coventry: NCET.

Collins, J., Hammond, M. and Wellington, J. (1997) *Teaching and Learning with Multimedia*. London: Routledge.

Cooper, P. and McIntyre, D. (1994) 'Patterns of interaction between teachers' and students' classroom thinking, and their implications for the provision of learning opportunities', *Teaching and Teacher Education*, **10** (6), 33–46.

Cortazzi, M. (1997) 'Classroom talk: communicating within the classroom relationship', in N. Kitson and R. Merry (eds) *Teaching in the Primary School*. London: Routledge.

Coupe-O'Kane, J., Porter, J. and Taylor, A. (1994) 'Meaningful content and contexts for learning', in J. Coupe-O'Kane and B. Smith (eds) *Taking Control: Enabling People with Learning Difficulties*. London: David Fulton.

Covington, M. V. (1998) *The Will to Learn: A Guide to Motivating Young People*. Cambridge: Cambridge University Press.

Creese, A., Norwich, B. and Daniels, H. (1998) 'The prevalence and usefulness of collaborative teacher groups for SEN: results of a national survey', *Support for Learning*, **13** (3), 109–114.

Crequer, N. (1996) *For Life: A Vision for Learning in the Twenty-first Century*. London: Campaign for Learning.

Darling-Hammond, L. (1996) 'The right to learn and the advancement of teaching: research, policy, and practice for democratic education', *Educational Researcher*, **25** (6), 5–17.

Davies, L. (1984) *Pupil Power: Deviance and Gender in School*. London: Falmer.

Day, C. (2000) 'Teachers in the twenty-first century: time to renew the vision (1)', *Teachers and Teaching: Theory and Practice*, **6** (1), 101–15.

Dearing, Sir R. (1996) *Review of Qualifications for 16 to 19-year-olds*. London: SCAA.

DES (1978) *Special Education Needs: Report of the Committee of Enquiry into the Education of Handicapped Children and Young Peoples* (The Warnock Report). London: HMSO.

DES (1990) Starting with Quality. Report of the Committee of Inquiry into the Quality of Educational Experience Offered to 3 and 4 Year Olds (The Rumbold Report). London: HMSO.

Delamont, S. (1983) *Interaction in the Classroom*. London: Methuen.

DfEE (1999a) *English National Curriculum*. Qualifications and Curriculum Authority, London: DfEE.

DfEE (1999b) *Permanent Exclusions from Schools in England 1997/98 and Exclusion Appeals Lodged by Parents in England 1997/98*: Statistical First Release 11/1999. London: DfEE.

DfEE Elton Report (1991) *Discipline in Schools*. London: HMSO.

Dewey, J. (1897) 'Knowledge as idealisation', in J. A. Boyston (ed.) (1970) *The Early Works of John Dewey: 1882–1898 Early Essays*. Carbondale, IL: Southern Illinois Press.

Dewey, J. (1938) *Experience and Education*. New York: Macmillan.

Dillon, J. T. (1994) *Using Discussions in Classrooms*. Buckingham: Open University Press.

Drummond, M. J. (1998) 'Children yesterday, today and tomorrow', in C. Richards and P. H. Taylor, *How Shall We School our Children? Primary Education and its Future*. London: Falmer.

Dunkin, M. J. and Biddle, B. J. (1974) *The Study of Teaching*. New York: Rinehart and Winston.

Dunst, C. J. and Trivette, C. M. (1986) 'Looking beyond the parent–child dyad for the determinants of maternal styles of interaction', *Infant Mental Health Journal*, **7**, 69–80.

Early Childhood Forum (1998) *Quality in Diversity: A Framework for Early Childhood Practitioners*. London: NCB.

Ecclestone, K. (1998) Care and Control: Defining Learners' Needs for Lifelong Learning. Paper presented to the British Educational Association Conference, Belfast, 27–30 August 1998.

Egglestone, J., Galton, M. and Jones, M. (1976) *Processes and Products of Science Teaching* (London: Macmillan), cited in S. Delamont (1983) *Interaction in the Classroom*. London: Methuen.

Entwistle, N. (1987) 'Motivation to learn: conceptualisations and practicalities', *British Journal of Educational Studies*, **35** (2), 129–48.

Ephraim, G. W. E. (1979) Developmental Process in Mental Handicap: A Generative Structure Approach. Unpublished PhD thesis, Brunel University.

Ewing, J. M. and Kennedy, E. M. (1996) 'Putting co-operative learning to good affect', *Reading*, **30** (1), 19–25.

Feldman, A. (1999) 'The role of conversation in collaborative action research', *Educational Action Research*, **7** (1), 125–44.

Felouzis, G. (1994) 'Le "bon prof": la construction de l'autorité dans les lycées', *Sociologie du Travail*, **36**, 361–76.

Ferguson, L. R. (1971) 'Origins of social development in infancy', *Merrill-Palmer Quarterly*, **17**, 119–39.

Field, T. M. (1977) 'Effects of early separation, interactive deficits and experimental manipulations on infant–mother face-to-face interaction', *Child Development*, **48**, 763–71.

Field, T. M. (1979) 'Games parents play with normal and high-risk infants', *Child Psychiatry and Human Development*, **10**, 41–8.

Fielding, M. (1997) 'Empowerment: emancipation or enervation?', in D. Bridges (ed.) *Education, Autonomy and Democratic Citizenship*. London: Routledge.

Fielding, M. (1999) 'Target setting, policy pathology and student perspectives: learning to labour in new times', *Cambridge Journal of Education*, **29** (2), 277–87.

Fogel, A. (1993) 'Two principles of communication: co-regulation and framing', in J. Nadel and L. Camaiomo (eds) *New Perspectives in Early Communication Development*. London: Routledge.

Fogelman, K. (1997) 'Education for Democratic Citizenship in Schools', in D. Bridges (ed.) *Education, Autonomy and Democratic Citizenship*. London: Routledge.

Forman, E. A. and Cazden, C. B. (1998) 'Exploring Vygotskian perspectives in education', in D. Faulkner, K. Littleton and M.

Woodhead (eds) *Learning Relationships in the Classroom*. London: Rout-ledge/Open University Press.

Foucault, M. (1980) *Power/Knowledge*. New York: Panthenon.

Freire, P. (1971) 'To the coordinator of a cultural circle', *Covergence*, **4** (1), 61–2.

Freire, P. (1972) *Pedagogy of the Oppressed*. Harmondsworth: Penguin.

Fryer, R. H. (1997) *Learning for the Twenty-first Century*. First Report of the National Advisory Group for Continuing Education and Life-long Learning. London: HMSO.

Gallas, K. (1998) *'Sometimes I Can Be Anything': Power, Gender and Identity in a Primary Classroom*. New York: Teachers College Press.

Gamson, Z. F. (1994) 'Collaborative learning comes of age', *Change*, **26** (5), 44–50.

Gardner, H. (1993) *Frames of Mind: The Theory of Multiple Intelligences*. London: Fontana.

Gardner, H. (1997) *Extraodinary Minds: Portraits of Exceptional Individuals and an Examination of our Extraordinariness*. London: Weidenfeld and Nicolson.

Giddens, A. (1991) *The Consequences of Modernity*. Cambridge: Polity.

Giroux, H. A. (1989) *Schooling for Democracy: Critical Pedagogy in the Modern Age*. London: Routledge.

Goduka, I. N. (1998) 'Educators as cultural awakeners and healers', *South African Journal of Higher Education*, **12** (2), 49–59.

Goffman, E. (1956) *The Presentation of Self in Everyday Life*. Edinburgh: University of Edinburgh Social Science Research Centre.

Goleman, D. (1996) *Emotional Intelligence: Why it Can Matter More than IQ*. London: Bloomsbury.

Grant, C. (1995) 'Unless I chose to tell you, you wouldn't know', in P. Potts, F. Armstrong and M. Masterton (eds) *Equality and Diversity in Education, Vol. 1: Learning, Teaching and Managing in Schools*. London: Routledge/Open University Press.

Greenhalgh, P. (1994) *Emotional Growth and Learning*. London: Routledge.

Greeno, J. G., Pearson, P. D. and Schoenfeld, A. H. (1999) 'Achieve-ment and theories of knowing and learning, in R. McCormick and C. Paechter, *Learning and Knowledge*. London: Paul Chapman.

Grice, P. (1975) 'Logic and conversation', in P. Cole and J. Morgan (eds) *Syntax and Semantics, Vol. III: Speech Acts*. New York: Academic Press.

Grove, N., Bunning, K., Porter, J. and Morgan, M. (2000) *See What I*

Mean: Guidelines to Aid Understanding of Communication by People with Severe and Profound Learning Disabilities. Kidderminster: British Institute of Learning Disabilities.

Grubb, W. N. (1999) *Honored but Invisible: An Inside Look at Teaching in Community Colleges.* London: Routledge.

Guntrip, H. (1949) *Psychology for Ministers and Social Workers.* London: Independent Press.

Guntrip, H. (1961) *Personality, Structure and Human Interaction.* London: Hogarth Press.

Guntrip, H. (1968) *Schizoid Phenomena, Object Relations and the Self.* London: The Hogarth Press.

Habermas, J. (1978) *Knowledge and Human Interests* (2nd edn). London: Heinemann.

Habermas, J. (1986) *Knowledge and Human Interests.* Cambridge, Polity Press.

Habermas, J. (1987) *The Philosophical Discourse of Modernity.* Cambridge: Polity Press.

Halsall, R. and Crockrett, M. (1998) 'Providing opportunities for active learning: assessing incidence and impact', *The Curriculum Journal*, **9** (3), 299–317.

Hansen, E. J. and Stephens, J. A. (2000) 'The ethics of learner-centred education', *Change*, **33** (5), 40–8.

Hanzlik, J. R. (1989) 'Interactions between mothers and their infants with developmental disabilities: analysis and review', *Physical and Occupational Therapy in Paediatrics*, **9**, 33–47.

Harding, C. (1983) 'Setting the stage for language acquisition: communication development in the first year', in R. Golinkoff (ed.) *The Transition from Pre-Linguistic to Linguistic Communication.* Hillsdale, NJ: Lawrence Erlbaum Associates.

Hargreaves, A. (1998) 'The emotional practice of teaching', *Teaching and Teacher Education*, **14** (8), 835–54.

Harkin, J. (1998a) 'Communication styles', *College Research*, Summer 1998, 40–3.

Harkin, J. (1998b) 'Constructs used by students in England and Wales to evaluate their teachers', *Journal of Vocational Education and Training*, **50** (3), 339–53.

Harkin, J. (1998c) 'In defence of the modernist project in education', *British Journal of Educational Studies*, **46** (4), 404–15.

Harkin, J. (1999) 'A European perspective: evaluating teaching quality in post-compulsory education', *College Research*, Autumn, **3** (1), 34.

Harkin, J. (2000) 'Participative education: an incomplete project of modernity', in C. Day and D. van Veen (eds) *Educational Research in Europe Yearbook 2000*. Leuven: Garant.

Harkin, J. and Davis, P. (1996) 'The impact of GNVQs on the communication styles of teachers', *Research in Post-compulsory Education*, **1** (1), 117–26.

Harkin, J., Davis, P. and Turner, G. (1999) 'The development of a communication styles questionnaire for use in English 16–19 education', *Westminster Studies in Education*, **22**, 31–47.

Harkin, J., Dawn, T. and Turner, G. (2001) *Teaching Young Adults*. London: Routledge.

Harré, R. (1998) *The Singular Self*. London: Sage.

Harrison, B. and Collins, J. (1998) 'Claiming and reclaiming an education: the experiences of multilingual school students in transition from primary to secondary school', *UNICORN, Journal of the Australian College of Education*, **24** (1), 16–29.

Harrison, B. T. (1976) A Literate Response. Unpublished PhD thesis, University of Exeter.

Hart, S. (1996) *Beyond Special Needs: Enhancing Children's Learning through Innovative Thinking*. London: Paul Chapman.

Haycock, K. and Navarro, M. S. (1988) *Unfinished Business: Fulfilling our Children's Promise* (Oakland, CA), cited in M. V. Covington (1998) *The Will to Learn: A Guide for Motivating Young People*. Cambridge: Cambridge University Press.

Heathcote. G. (1997) 'Developing personal autonomy in continuing professional development', in D. Bridges (ed.) *Education, Autonomy and Democratic Citizenship*. London: Routledge.

Hewett, D. and Nind, M. (1998) (eds) *Interaction in Action: Reflections on the Use of Intensive Interaction*. London: David Fulton.

Hoban, G. (1999) 'The role of community in action learning: a Deweyian perspective on sharing experiences, in J. Retallick, B. Cocklin and K. Coombe (eds) *Learning Communities in Education*. London: Routledge.

Hockley, M. and Harkin, J. (2000) 'Communicating with students with learning difficulties in further education', *Educational Action Research*, **8** (2), 341–60.

Hodapp, R. M. and Goldfield, E. C. (1983) 'The use of mother–infant games with delayed children', *Early Child Development and Care*, **13**, 17–32.

Hodgson, A. and Spours, K. (2001) *Improving the 'Use' Value of Key Skills: Debating the Role of the Key Skills Qualification within Curriculum 2000*. IOE/Nuffield Series Report 4. London: Institute of Education.

Hollingsworth, S. (1994) *Teacher Research and Urban Literacy Education: Lessons and conversations in a feminist key.* New York: Teachers College Press.

Holloway, G. (1995) 'All change: accreditation and "other" learners', in M. Stuart and A. Thomson, (1995).

hooks, b. (1994) *Teaching to Transgress.* London: Routledge.

Horn, S. K. (1997) 'Idea in practice: extending collaboration beyond the developmental classrooom', *Journal of Developmental Education,* **21** (2), 26–32.

Hughes, M. and Westgate, D. (1997) 'Assistants as talk partners in early-years classrooms: some issues of support and development', *Educational Review,* **49**, 5–12.

Hutchens, D. (1998) *Outlearning the Wolves: Surviving and Thriving in a Learning Organization.* Waltham, MA: Pegasus.

ILEA (1985) *The Fish Report.* London: ILEA.

Ilgen, D. R., Fisher, C. D. and Taylor, M. S. (1979) 'Consequences of individual feedback on behaviour in organisations', *Journal of Applied Psychology,* **64**, 39–71.

Indoe, D., Leo, E., James, J. and Charlton, T. (1992) 'Developing your "self" and others: the EASI way', *Educational Psychology in Practice,* **8** (3), 151–5.

Jackson, M. (2000) 'Introduction', in L. Brigham, D. Atkinson, M. Jackson, S. Rolph and J. Walmsley (eds) *Crossing Boundaries: Change and Continuity in the History of Learning Disability.* Kidderminster: British Institute of Learning Disabilities.

Johannessen, T., Gronhaug, K., Risholm, N. and Mikalsen, O. (1997) 'What is important to students? Exploring dimensions in their evaluations of teachers', *Scandinavian Journal of Educational Research,* **41** (2), 165–77.

Johnson, D. W. and Johnson, R. T. (1987) *Learning Together and Alone: Cooperative, Competitive and Individualistic Learning* (2nd edn). NJ: Prentice-Hall.

Johnson, N. (1999) 'Becoming learning communities', in J. Retallick, B. Cocklin and K. Coombe (eds) *Learning Communities in Education.* London: Routledge.

Kansanen, P. (1999) 'Teaching as teaching-studying-learning interaction', *Scandinavian Journal of Educational Research,* **43** (1), 81–9.

Kant, E. (1949) [1782] 'Groundwork of the Metaphysics of Morals', in H. J. Paton (ed.) *The Moral Law.* London: Hutchinson.

Kinder, K., Harland, J., Wilkin, A. and Wakefield, A. (1995) *Three to Remember: Strategies for Disaffected Pupils.* Slough: NFER.

Kingman, Sir J. (1988) *Report of the Committee of Enquiry into the Teaching of the English Language*. London: HMSO.

Knott, L. (1998) 'Ben's story: developing the communication abilities of a pupil with autism', in D. Hewett and M. Nind (eds) *Interaction in Action: Reflections on the Use of Intensive Interaction*. London: David Fulton.

Krevesky, M. and Seidel, S. (1998) 'Minds at work: applying multiple intelligences in the classroom', in R. J. Sternberg and W. M. Williams (eds) *Intelligence, Instruction and Assessment: Theory into Practice*. Mahwah, NJ: Lawrence Erlbaum Associates.

Lakoff, R. (1977) 'The logic of politeness or minding your p's and q's', in A. K. Pugh, V. J. Lee and J. Swann (eds) *Language and Language Use*. Oxford: Heinemann.

Laing, R. D. (1959) *The Divided Self*. London: Tavistock.

Lawley, J. (1999) 'A journey towards an understanding of learning', *The Journal of the 21st Century Learning Initiative*, May 1999, 8–16.

Lawrence, D. (1985) 'Improving reading and self-esteem', *Educational Research*, **27** (3), 194–200.

Lawrence, D. (1988) *Enhancing Self-Esteem in the Classroom*. London: Paul Chapman.

Leary, T. (1957) *An Interpersonal Diagnosis of Personality*. New York: Ronald Press Company.

LeDoux, J. (1998) *The Emotional Brain*. London: Weidenfeld and Nicolson.

Lewis, C. and O'Brian, M. (1987) *Reassessing Fatherhood*. London: Sage.

Lewis, M. and Goldberg, S. (1969) 'Perceptual–cognitive development in infancy: a generalized expectancy model as a function of the mother–infant interaction', *Merrill-Palmer Quarterly*, **15**, 81–100.

Lunenburg, M. L. and Volman, M. (1999) 'Active learning: views and actions of students and teachers in basic education', *Teaching and Teacher Education*, **15**, 431–45.

McCabe, T. (1981) 'Schools and careers: for girls who do want to wear the trousers', in A. McRobbie and T. McCabe (eds) *Feminism for Girls: An Adventure Story*. London: Routledge and Kegan Paul.

McCollum, J. A. (1984) 'Social interaction between babies and parents: validation of an intervention procedure', *Child Care Health and Development*, **10**, 301–15.

McDermott, R. P. (1996) [First published 1993] 'The acquisition of a child by a learning disability', in S. Chaikin and J. Lave, *Understand-*

ing Practice: Perspectives on Activity and Context. Cambridge: Cambridge University Press.

McGee, J. J., Menolscino, F. J., Hobbs, D. C. and Menousek, P. E. (1987) *Gentle Teaching: A Nonaversive Approach for Helping Persons with Mental Retardation*. New York: Human Science Press.

Malinowski, B. (1935) *The Language and Magic of Gardening*. London: Allen & Unwin.

Marfo, K. (1991) 'The maternal directiveness theme in mother–infant interaction research: implications for early intervention', in K. Marfo (ed.) *Early Intervention in Transition: Current Perspectives on Programs for Handicapped Children*. New York: Praeger.

Mercer, N. (1995) *The Guided Construction of Knowledge: Talk amongst Teachers and Learners*. Clevedon: Multilingual Matters.

Michaels, S. and Collins, J. (1984) 'Oral discourse style: classroom interaction and the acquisition of literacy', in D. Tannen (ed.) *Coherence in Written and Spoken Discourse*. Norwood, NJ: Ablex.

Mittler, P. (2000) *Working towards Inclusive Education: Social Contexts*. London: David Fulton.

Moll, L. C. and Whitmore, K. F. (1998) 'Vygotsky in classroom practice: moving from individual transmission to social interaction', in D. Faulkner, K. Littleton and M. Woodhead (eds), *Learning Relationships in the Classroom*. London: Routledge/Open University Press.

Munn, P., Lloyd, G. and Cullen, M. A. (2000) *Alternatives to School Exclusion*. London: Paul Chapman.

Murray, P. (2000) 'Disabled children, parents and professionals: partnership in whose terms?' *Disability and Society*, **15** (4), 638–98.

National Curriculum Council (1989) *Arts in Schools Project*. London: HMSO.

Naysmith, J. and Palma, A. (1998) 'Teachers talking, teachers reflecting: how do teachers reflect on their practice? A case study', *Teachers and Teaching: Theory and Practice*, **4** (1), 65–76.

Nias, J. (1996) 'Thinking about feeling: the emotions in teaching', *Cambridge Journal of Education*, **26** (3), 293–306.

Nind, M. (1996) 'Efficacy of Intensive Interaction: developing sociability and communication in people with severe learning difficulties using an approach based on caregiver–infant interaction', *European Journal of Special Needs Education*, **11** (1), 48–66.

Nind, M. (1999) 'Intensive interaction and autism: a useful approach?', *British Journal of Special Education*, **26** (2), 96–102.

Nind, M. (2000) 'Teachers' understanding of interactive approaches in special education', *International Journal of Disability, Development and Education*, **47** (2), 183–99.

Nind, M. and Cochrane, S. (in press) 'Inclusive curricula? Pupils on the margins of special schools', *International Journal of Inclusive Education*.

Nind, M. and Hewett, D. (1988) 'Interaction as curriculum: a process method in a school for pupils with severe learning difficulties', *British Journal of Special Education*, **15**, 55–7.

Nind, M. and Hewett, D. (1994) *Access to Communication: Developing the Basics of Communication with People with Severe Learning Difficulties through Intensive Interaction*. London: David Fulton.

Nind, M. and Hewett, D. (1996) 'When age-appropriateness isn't appropriate', in J. Coupe-O'Kane and J. Goldbart (eds) *Whose Choice? Contentious Issues for those Working with People with Learning Difficulties*. London: David Fulton.

Nind, M. and Hewett, D. (2001) *A Practical Guide to Intensive Interaction*. Kidderminster: British Institute of Learning Disabilities.

Nind, M. and Powell, S. (2000) 'Intensive interaction and autism: some theoretical concerns', *Children and Society*, **14** (2), 98–109.

Nind, M., Kellett, M. and Hopkins, V. (2001) 'Teachers' talk styles: communication with learners with severe learning difficulties', *Child Language, Teaching and Therapy*, **17** (2), 1–17.

Noddings, N. (1996) 'Stories and affect in teacher education', *Cambridge Journal of Education*, **26** (3), 435–47.

O'Keffe, D. J. (1994) *Truancy in English Secondary Schools*. London: HMSO.

Oakeshott, M. (1959) *The Voice of Poetry in the Conversation of Mankind*. London: Bowes & Bowes.

OBESSU (1996) Vocational Education and Training Conference and Network, obessu@obessu.org

OECD (1978) *Report of the Centre for Educational Research and Innovation*. Paris: OECD.

OECD (1996) *Lifelong Learning for All*. Meeting of the Education Committee at ministerial level, 16–17 January 1996. Paris: OECD.

Ogilvy, C. M., Boath, E. H., Cheyne, W. M., Jahoda, G. and Schaffer, H. R. (1992) 'Staff–child interaction styles in multi-ethnic nursery schools', *British Journal of Developmental Psychology*, **10**, 85–97.

Open University (2001) *E842: Developing Practice in Primary Education: Study Guide*. Milton Keynes: Open University.

Outhwaite, W. (1994) *Habermas: A Critical Introduction*. Cambridge: Polity Press.

Oxfam International (1999) *Education Now: Break the Cycle of Poverty*. Oxford: Oxfam Publications.

Parsons, C. (1999) *Education, Exclusion and Citizenship*. London: Routledge.

Popper, K. (1972) *Objective Knowledge*. Oxford: Oxford University Press.

Powell, S. (2000a) 'Conclusion: towards a pedagogy for autism', in S. Powell (ed.) *Helping Children with Autism to Learn*. London: David Fulton.

Powell, S. (2000b) 'Learning about life asocially: the autistic perspective on education', in S. Powell (ed.) *Helping Children with Autism to Learn*. London: David Fulton.

Preece, J. (2000) 'Challenging the discourses of inclusion and exclusion with off-limits curricula', *Working Papers of the Global Colloquium on Supporting Lifelong Learning* (online). Milton Keynes: Open University. Available from http://www.open.ac/lifelong-learning [accessed 28 September 2001].

Reay, D. and Wiliam, D. (1999) ' "I'll be a nothing": structure, agency and the construction of identity through assessment', *British Educational Research Journal*, **25** (3), 343–54.

Reddy, M. J. (1979) 'The conduit metaphor: a case of frame conflict in our language about language', in A. Ortony (ed.) *Metaphor and Thought*. Cambridge: Cambridge University Press.

Retallick, J. (1999) 'Transforming schools into learning communities', in J. Retallick, B. Cocklin, and K. Coombe (eds) *Learning Communities in Education*. London: Routledge.

Richardson, R. (1990) *Daring to Be a Teacher*. Stoke-on-Trent: Trentham Books.

Rodenburg, P. (1992) *The Right to Speak*. London: Methuen.

Rogers, C. (1983) *Freedom to Learn for the 80's*. New York: Macmillan.

Rogoff, B. (1999) 'Cognitive development through social interaction: Vygotsky and Piaget', in P. Murphy (ed.) *Learners, Learning and Assessment*. London: Paul Chapman.

Sameroff, A. (1975) 'Transactional models in early social interactions', *Human Development*, **18**, 65–79.

Schaffer, H. R. (1971) *The Growth of Sociability*. Harmondsworth: Penguin.

Schaffer, H. R. (1977) (ed.) *Studies in Mother–Infant Interaction*. London: Academic Press.

Schaffer, H. R. (1984) *The Child's Entry into the Social World*. New York: Academic Press.

Searle, J. (1992) 'Conversation', in H. Parret and J. Verschueren (eds) *Searle on Conversation*. Philadelphia: John Benjamin.

Seligman, M. (1975) *Helplessness: On Depression, Development and Death.* San Francisco: Freeman.

Senge, P. M. (1990) *The Fifth Discipline: The Art and Practice of the Learning Organization.* New York: Currency Doubleday.

Senge, P. M., Kleiner, A., Roberts, C., Ross, R. B. and Smith, B. J. (1994). *The Fifth Discipline Field Book: Strategies and Tools for Building a Learning Organization.* New York: Currency Doubleday.

Sergiovanni, T. (1999) 'The story of community', in J. Retallick, B. Cocklin and K. Coombe (eds) *Learning Communities in Education.* London: Routledge.

Sergiovanni, T. J. and Starratt, R. J. (1988) *Supervision Human Perspectives* (4th edn). New York: McGraw-Hill.

Shor, I. (1993) 'Education is politics: Paulo Freire's critical pedagogy', in P. McLaren and P. Leonard (eds) *Paulo Freire: A Critical Encounter.* London: Routledge.

Shotter, J. (1973) 'Aquired powers: the transformation of natural into personal powers', *Journal for the Theory of Social Behaviour,* **3** (2), 141–56.

Sinclair, J. (1992) 'Bridging the gaps: an inside-out view of autism', in E. Schopler and G. Mesibov (eds) *The High Functioning Individual with Autism.* New York: Plenum Press.

Sloboda, J., Davidson, J. W. and Howe, M. A. J. (1999) 'Is everyone musical?', in P. Murphy (ed.) *Learners, Learning and Assessment.* London: Paul Chapman.

Smith, B. (1989) 'Which approach? The education of pupils with SLD', *Mental Handicap,* **17**, 111–15.

Smith, C. (1998) 'Jamie's story: intensive interaction in a college of further education', in Hewett, D. and Nind, M. (eds) *Interaction In Action: Reflections on the Use of Intensive Interaction.* London: David Fulton.

Smith, F. (1978) *Reading.* Cambridge: Cambridge University Press.

Smith-Livdahl, B., Smart, K., Wallman, J., Herbert, T., Geiger, D. K. and Anderson, J. L. (1995) *Stories from Response-centered Classrooms: Speaking, Questioning and Theorizing from the Center of the Action.* New York: Teachers College Press.

Snow, C. E. (1976) 'The development of conversation between mothers and babies', *Journal of Child Language,* **4**, 1–22.

Social Exclusion Unit (1998) *Truancy and Social Exclusion Report.* London: Social Exclusion Unit.

Stainback, S. and Stainback, W. (1996) *Inclusion: a guide for educators.* Baltimore: Powl H. Brookes.

Starratt, R. J. (1996) *Transforming Educational Administration: Meaning, Community and Excellence*. New York: McGraw-Hill.

Stenhouse, L. (1967) *Culture and Education*. London: Nelson.

Stern, D. N. (1974) 'Mother and infant at play: the dyadic interaction involving facial, vocal and gaze behaviours', in M. Lewis and L. A. Rosenblum (eds) *The Effect of the Infant on its Caregiver*. New York: Wiley.

Stern, D. N., Beebe, B., Jaffe, J. and Bennett, S. L. (1977) 'The infant's stimulus world during social interaction: a study of caregiver behaviours with particular reference to repetition and timing', in H. R. Schaffer (ed.) *Studies in Mother–Infant Interaction*. London: Academic Press.

Stevenson, Robert B. (1990) 'Engagement and cognitive challenge in thoughtful social studies classes: a study of student perspectives', *Journal of Curriculum Studies*, **22** (4), 329–41.

Stuart, M. (1995a) ' "If experience counts, then why am I bothering to come here?": AP(E)L and learning', in M. Stuart and A. Thomson, *op. cit.*

Stuart, M. (1995b) 'Introduction: engaging with difference: education and "other" adults', in M. Stuart and A. Thomson, *op. cit.*

Stuart, M. and Thomson, A. (eds) (1995) *Engaging with Difference: The 'Other' in Adult Education*. Leicester: National Organization for Learning.

Stubbs, M. (1976) *Language, Schools and Classrooms*. London: Methuen.

Thiong'o, Ngugi wa (1977) *Petals of Blood*. London: Cox & Wyman.

Thomas, G. and Loxley, A. (2001) *Deconstructing Special Education and Constructing Inclusion*. Buckingham: Open University Press.

Tinto, V. and Goodsell-Love, A. (1993) 'Building community', *Liberal Education*, **79** (4), 16–22.

Turnbull. C. (1973) *Africa and Change*. New York: Knopf.

van Lier, L. (1996) *Interaction in the Language Curriculum*. London: Longman.

von Glasersfeld, E. (1995) *Radical Constructivism: A Way of Knowing and Learning*. London: Falmer.

von Tezchner, S. (1996) 'Facilitated, automatic and false communication: current issues in the use of facilitating techniques', *European Journal of Special Needs Education*, **11**, 151–66.

Vygotsky, L. S. (1962) *Thought and Language* (ed. and trans. by E. Hanfmann and G. Vahar). Cambridge, MA: MIT.

Vygotsky, L. S. (1978) 'Mind in society: the development of higher psychological processes', in M. Cole, V. John-Steiner, S. Scribner and E. Souberman (eds and translators) Cambridge, MA: Harvard University Press.

Wade, B. and Moore, M. (1993) *Experiencing Special Needs*. Buckingham: Open University Press.

Ware, J. (1996) *Creating a Responsive Environment for People with Profound and Multiple Learning Difficulties*. London: David Fulton.

Warren, S. F. and Rogers-Warren, A. (1984) 'The social basis of language and communication in severely handicapped preschoolers', *Topics in Early Childhood Special Education*, **4**, 57–72.

Watson, J. (2000) 'Constructive instruction and learning difficulties', *Support for Learning*, **15** (3), 134–40.

Weiner, G. (1985) (ed.) *Just a Bunch of Girls*. Milton Keynes: Open University Press.

Weistuch, L. and Byers-Brown, B. (1987) 'Motherese as therapy: a programme and its dissemination', *Child Language Teaching and Therapy*, **3**, 57–71.

Wells, P. (1999) 'Different and equal: fostering interdependence in a learning community', in J. Retallick, B. Cocklin and K. Coombe (eds), *Learning Communities in Education*. London: Routledge.

Wenger, E. (1998) *Communities of Practice: Learning, Meaning and Identity*. Cambridge: Cambridge University Press.

Westgate, D. and Hughes, M. (1997) 'Identifying "quality" in classroom talk: an enduring research task', *Language and Education*, **11** (2), 125–39.

Willes, M. J. (1983) *Children into Pupils: A Study of Language in Early Schooling*. London: Routledge.

Williams, D. (1996) *Autism: An Inside-Out Approach*. London: Jessica Kingsley.

Williams, L. and Nind, M. (1999) 'Insiders or outsiders: normalisation and women with learning difficulties', *Disability and Society*, **14** (5), 659–72.

Wilkinson, A. (1968) 'The implications of oracy', *Educational Review*, **20** (5).

Wilkinson, A. (1975) *Language and Education*. Oxford: Oxford University Press.

Winnicott, D. W. (1986) *Home Is Where We Start from*. Harmondsworth: Penguin.

Wood, D., Bruner, J. S. and Ross, G. (1976) 'The role of tutoring in problem-solving', *Journal of Child Psychology and Psychiatry*, **17**, 89–100.

Woodhead, M. (1999) 'Quality in early childhood programmes – a contextually appropriate approach', in B. Moon and P. Murphy (eds) *Curriculum in Context*. London: Paul Chapman.

Wubbels, T. and Levy, J. (1993) (eds) *Do You Know What You Look Like? Interpersonal Relationships in Education*. London: Falmer.

www.notschool.net

www.learnwebharvard.edu/ent

www.transform.org

Yoder, P. J. (1990) 'The theoretical and empirical basis of early amelioration of developmental disabilities: implications for future research', *Journal of Early Intervention*, **14**, 27–42.

Young, R. (1991) *A Critical Theory of Education: Habermas and our Children's Future*. Hemel Hempstead: Harvester Wheatsheaf.

Young, R. (1992) *Critical Theory and Classroom Talk*. Clevedon: Multilingual Matters.

Index